Development

economics

Frederick Nixson
Professor of Development Economics
University of Manchester

Series Editor
Bryan Hurl
Harrow School

Heinemann Educational Publishers
Halley Court, Jordan Hill, Oxford OX2 8EJ
a division of Reed Educational & Professional Publishing Ltd
MELBOURNE   AUCKLAND   OXFORD
CHICAGO   PORTSMOUTH (NH)   BLANTYRE
IBADAN   GABORONE   JOHANNESBURG

© Frederick Nixson, 1996

First published 1996

00 99
10 9 8 7 6 5

British Library Cataloguing in Publication Data

A catalogue record for this book is available from the British Library

ISBN 0 435 33033 0

Typeset and illustrated by TechType, Abingdon, Oxon
Printed and bound in Great Britain by Biddles Ltd, Guildford and King's Lynn

Acknowledgements

The publishers would like to thank the following for the use of copyright material:

Associated Examining Board for the questions on pp. 71, 87; © *The Economist*, London, 5 April 1995 on p. 14, 1 October, 1994 on p. 35, 2 October 1993 on pp. 58–60, 10 December 1994 on p. 85; *Financial Times* for the extract on p. 77; *The Guardian* on pp. 37–8 and 87–8; McGraw-Hill for the extract adapted from *Economics* by D. Begg, S. Fisher and R. Dornbusch, 1987 on p. 72; Newspaper Publishing plc for the article from *The Independent* on pp. 8–9; Northern Examinations and Assessment Board for the questions on pp. 21, 36, 49, 58; Overseas Development Institute for the figure from 'Commodity Prices: Investing in Decline?', ODI *Briefing Paper*, March 1988 on p. 63; Oxford and Cambridge Schools Examination Board for the questions on pp. 71, 87; Oxford University Press for the figure 'Burkino Faso - Locked in Deprivation' from *The State of the World's Children* (Unicef), 1995 on p. 8; Oxford University Press Inc. for 'The East-Asian Miracle' adapted from *The East Asian Miracle: Economic Growth and Public Policy*, 1993 on p. 55 and for "The Uruguay Round, Market Access, and the Developing Countries' from the *World Bank Annual Report* by the World Bank on p. 64; Organization for Economic Cooperation and Development for the table on p. 81; Prentice-Hall/Harvester Wheatshef, Hemel Hempstead for the table from '*Economics of Change in Less Developed Countries*', Colman/Nixson, 1994 on p. 15; the United Nations for the table from 'United Nations Global Outlook 2000: An Economic, Social and Environmental Perspective', United Nations Publications, 1990 on p. 52 and the tables from 'The World Investment Report: Transnational Corporations as Engines of Growth', New York 1992 on pp. 74 and 75; United Nations Development Fund for the articles on pp. 16 and 21–2, and the tables on pp. 17, 18, 33 and 41; United Nations Industrial Development Organization for the statistics on p. 53; University of Cambridge Local Examinations Syndicate for the questions on p. 7, 21–2, 31, 36, 57, 71, 79, 87; University of London Examinations & Assessment Council for the questions on p. 8–9, 20, 37–8, 49, 58–60, 72, 87–8; the World Bank for data on pp. 6, 19, 34, 42, 45, 84, 86.

The publishers have made every attempt to contact the correct copyright holders. However, if any material has been incorrectly attributed, we will be happy to correct this at the earliest opportunity.

Contents

Preface

Until recently writers of textbooks have neglected the topic of development economics, but many are now deciding to include a chapter on it as newer editions are produced. Such efforts unfortunately tend to look suspiciously superficial – somewhat like an A level 'fashion accessory', or a figleaf to cover up embarrassing deficiencies.

In contrast, as Frederick Nixson is an acknowledged expert on development economics, this new book covers the subject comprehensively to the standard required for the most recent syllabuses offered by the University of Cambridge Local Examinations Syndicate and the University of London Examinations and Assessment Council.

Bryan Hurl
Series Editor

Introduction

Developing countries cover more than two-thirds of the Earth's land surface and by the year 2000 they will account for more than four-fifths of the world's population. Over 150 countries are variously classified as low- or middle-income, newly industrializing or petroleum exporting, and they vary greatly in size, structure, level of development – especially with respect to their level of industrialization, history and culture.

To attempt to capture and explain this diversity in a short book is ambitious. But development economists believe that common elements can be found and useful generalizations made. The economist provides one part of the explanation of poverty, growth and development, using ideas and concepts drawn from orthodox economic analysis and new concepts and techniques drawn from the study of poor countries themselves. Other social scientists – sociologists, political scientists, geographers – help to complete the explanation.

This book is thus an introduction to a huge subject – the study of economic development.

- Chapter 1 gives an overview of the dimensions of *global poverty* and considers the different ways by which poverty can be measured.
- Chapter 2 discusses the notion of *development*, distinguishing it from *economic growth*; highlights problems of measurement; and outlines the *human development index* as an example of a *composite indicator* of development.
- Chapter 3 surveys *development theory*. The original theoretical contributions of development economists are noted and alternative theoretical perspectives discussed.
- Chapter 4 places the discussion of development within the broader *global context*. Developing countries in the 1980s were subject to a series of unprecedented *external shocks* from which many of them have found it difficult to recover.
- Chapter 5 returns to a central concern of development – the *distribution of income* in poor countries. The possible link between more rapid economic growth and greater income inequality is noted, but it is emphasized that there is no single economic model linking growth and equity.
- Chapter 6 is concerned with *population* and *the environment*. Both topics are important in their own right but they are linked together closely in the development process.
- Chapter 7 focuses on *agricultural* and *industrial development* and highlights the rise of the *Newly Industrializing Economies* (NIEs).

1

The latter return us to the question of different theoretical perspectives and this highlights conflicting notions of the role of the state in the development process.

- Chapter 8 considers *international trade* in more detail, with particular attention focused on the *terms of trade* of poor, primary commodity exporting countries.
- Chapter 9 discusses the role of *transnational corporations* (TNCs) in development, and some conflicts of interest between TNCs and host countries are noted.
- Chapter 10 concludes the book with a discussion of the issues relating to *aid* and *debt*. The complexity of both the *aid relationship* and the *debt crisis* is emphasized, and the changing roles of the *World Bank* and *International Monetary Fund* are noted.

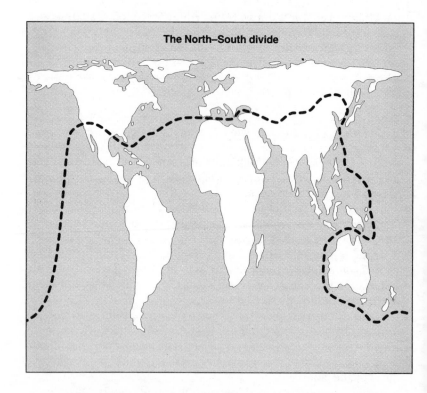

The North–South divide

A NOTE ON TERMINOLOGY

The poor countries of the world are referred to by a variety of terms – under-developed, less developed, developing, the Third World, the South.

The developed market (capitalist) economies – the **'First World'** – are seen as forming the core of the global economy. The poor countries – the 'Third World' – constitute a dependent periphery.

The former 'Second World' – the centrally planned command economies of Eastern and Central Europe and the former Soviet Union (FSU), are now referred to as **'transitional economies',** in the process of moving from a planned to a free market economy.

Some poorer economies with socialist development objectives – Tanzania, Mozambique, Laos, Mongolia, for example – have abandoned those objectives and have implemented economic and political reforms. Others, such as China and Vietnam, have not formally abandoned their socialist development objectives but have implemented massive reform programmes such that the market mechanism, and not the plan, is the main allocator of resources.

Two socialist economies – Cuba, North Korea – continue to resist change. Elsewhere we see the emergence of the **Newly Industrializing Economies (NIEs)** – South Korea, Taiwan, Singapore and Hong Kong, the original 'Gang of Four', and Malaysia, Thailand and Indonesia. At the other end of the income spectrum, the United Nations' Conference on Trade and Development (UNCTAD) categorizes 48 of the poorest countries as 'least developed'.

Use of all the above terminology gives rise to problems.

- If we refer to poor countries as 'less' or 'under' or 'least' developed, we must pose the question – with respect to what? Implicitly we are comparing these economies and their levels of development to the developed market economies and the latter thus become a 'model' for poor countries to copy. This may not be appropriate, however, given that poor countries may wish to pursue development objectives that are different from those represented by developed market economies.
- More importantly, it may not be possible to replicate the experience of the developed market economy. We can draw lessons from the experience of other countries (although history does not repeat itself) and each country must define its own path to development.
- The notion of a 'Third World' is also misleading. It implies a separateness from the 'First World' which does not in fact exist. Poor countries are linked in a variety of ways to the developed market economies – through trade, financial flows, and cultural and military links – and thus development and growth in poor countries is in part determined by decisions taken in developed economies.

Chapter One

Poverty: the global dimensions

'What is vital for the health of our global society today is that governments and citizens set their forces towards global poverty eradication.' Oxfam, 1995

In 1985, the World Bank estimated that more than 1.1 billion people in the developing world were living in **poverty**, defined as the *'inability to attain a minimal standard of living'*.

To make this definition of poverty useful, three questions must be answered:

- How do we measure the standard of living?
- What is meant by a minimal standard of living?
- Having identified the poor, how can the extent of poverty be expressed in a single measure or index?

Measuring the standard of living

Household incomes and expenditures *per capita* are most commonly used to provide a quantitatively defined standard of poverty and to make comparisons between different countries or regions. Such measures do not, however, include such aspects of **welfare** as health, life expectancy, literacy and access to **public goods** (clean drinking water, for example). Because of these weaknesses, *consumption-based poverty measures* are used as a measure of well-being.

The poverty line

All measures of poverty relate to a given norm or average, and the consumption-based poverty line comprises two elements:

- the expenditure necessary to buy a minimum standard of nutrition and other basic necessities, and
- *'a further amount that varies from country to country, reflecting the cost of participating in the everyday life of society'* (World Bank).

The first element can be calculated in a straightforward manner. The cost of minimum adequate caloric intakes and other necessities is estimated from the prices of the goods that constitute the consumption bundles of the poor. The second element, however, is subjective and varies with *per capita* income – that is, the *richer* a country is, the *higher* is its poverty line.

Poverty can thus be viewed as either an *absolute* or a *relative* concept. The World Bank bases its estimates of poverty on the absolute concept and uses two 'global poverty lines' – US$370 and $275 per person per year (measured in constant 1985 purchasing power parity prices).

How much poverty is there?

Using the *headcount method*, and adopting the upper poverty line – US$370 – gives the above-quoted estimate of 1.1 billion poor people in developing countries in poverty in 1985, approximately one-third of their total population. Adopting the lower poverty line – US$275 – gives a figure of 630 million, approximately 18 per cent of developing country population.

Table 1 illustrates the distribution of poverty by region. Nearly one-half of the developing world's poor live in South Asia. Sub-Saharan Africa has fewer poor people, but as a percentage of total population (the 'headcount index') its poverty is roughly as great. China in 1985 had a large number of poor people but a relatively low headcount index, in part reflecting the Chinese government's emphasis on job creation, the provision of rural health facilities, effective distribution of food to both cities and countryside, and a general guarantee of social security.

Poverty is usually worse in rural than in urban areas, as is malnutrition, lack of education and poor housing. The extent of poverty varies among rural areas, however, with the poor located in regions where arable land tends to be scarce, agricultural productivity is low, and drought, floods and environmental degradation are common.

In urban areas the poor typically live in slums or squatter settlements and suffer from overcrowding, poor or non-existent sanitation facilities, and contaminated water supplies. Poor households tend to be large, although it is not clear if households are poor because they are large or large because they are poor (that is, it is essential to have large numbers of children to ensure that some survive to support the household when parents are old). Either way, poor children are vulnerable to disease and malnutrition and poverty-related illnesses can cause permanent damage. Women, too, are disproportionately represented among the poor and are severely disadvantaged with respect to health, nutrition, education and employment.

Table 1 Poverty in the developing countries in 1985 (Source: World Bank)

Region	Extremely poor		Poor (including extremely poor)		Social indicators		
	Number (millions)	Headcount index (%)	Number (millions)	Headcount index (%)	Under-5 mortality (per thousand)	Life expectancy (years)	Net primary enrolment rate (%)
Sub-Saharan Africa	120	30	180	47	196	50	56
East Asia	120	9	280	20	96	67	96
China	80	8	210	20	58	69	93
South Asia	300	29	520	51	172	56	74
India	250	33	420	55	199	57	81
Eastern Europe	3	4	6	8	23	71	90
Middle East and North Africa	40	21	60	31	148	61	75
Latin America and Caribbean	50	12	70	19	75	66	92
All developing countries	633	18	1116	33	121	62	83

Note: The poverty line in 1985 PPP dollars is $275 *per capita* a year for the extremely poor and $370 *per capita* a year for the poor. The headcount index is defined as the percentage of the population below the poverty line.

Eradication of poverty:
global cooperation and national commitment

No one doubts the urgency of the need to alleviate, and ultimately eliminate, global poverty. But rhetoric is not always matched by action and deep divisions of opinion remain as to how problems of poverty can best be tackled.

On the one hand, there are those countries and institutions (the USA and the World Bank, for example) that argue for pro-market policies, emphasizing the liberalization of the economy and minimal state intervention. Emphasis is placed on agricultural development, employment creation through the use of labour-intensive technologies, and investment in health and education to raise the quality of human capital (**human resource development**).

While not denying the importance of such policies, other institutions, including the UN family and development-related institutions, and more radical political leaders, emphasize the importance of global factors which trap poor countries in a poverty cycle and make their escape from poverty difficult, if not impossible. Low commodity prices, poor trading opportunities, already inadequate and falling real values of official development assistance (aid) and the debt crisis all point to the need to transform the global economy and its institutions in order to give **Third World** countries a better deal.

KEY WORDS

Poverty	Poverty line
Standard of living	Human resource development
Welfare	Third World
Public goods	

Essay topics

1. On what basis and with what confidence might an economist say that living standards are higher in some countries than others? [University of Cambridge Local Examinations Syndicate 1993]

2. Explain how economists measure living standards in an economy and discuss the possible uses which could be made of this information. [20 marks]
   [University of Cambridge Local Examinations Syndicate, AS level, 1995]

Data Response Question

This task is based on a question set in a specimen paper by the University of London Examinations and Assessment Council. Read the article entitled 'Looking for a road out of nowhere', by H. McRae, which appeared in the *Independent on Sunday* on 19 February 1995. Then answer the questions.

Burkina Faso – locked in deprivation

Population	9.8 million
Economic growth rate 1980–92	1% per annum
Population growth rate 1980–93	2.6% per annum
Under five infant mortality rate	175 per 1,000 (UK = 8)
Life expectancy at birth	48 years
Adult literacy rate	18%
Babies with low birth weight	21%
People with access to health care	51%
People with access to safe water	56%
Boys in primary school	36%
Girls in primary school	23%

Source: *The State of the World's Children 1995,* published by OUP for Unicef.

Burkina Faso, formerly Upper Volta, is undoubtedly very poor. It is not the poorest country in the world – its income of $300 per head a year puts it well ahead of countries such as Mozambique or Ethiopia. But in the UNDP's 1993 Human Development Report is ranked 170 out of 173 countries, with only Afghanistan, Sierra Leone and Guinea behind it.

But it does not feel like a disaster zone: just that life for most people is very precarious. That may be something to do with the good rains last summer. Or it may be that poverty in the countryside (and Burkina Faso is exceptionally rural, with only 18 per cent of its population in towns) always seems less gnawing than urban poverty.

What does feel quite extraordinary – and gives a measure of the poverty – is the lack of cars. An apparently prosperous town of 2000 or 3000 people will have not a single private car. There is hardly a petrol pump between Ouagadougou and Po, 100 miles to the south on the Ghana border, and not a working one in Po itself.

The area is not a disaster zone – yet. The population will double in the next generation, raising the brutal question as to how this country can manage to feed, clothe and house these extra people. It cannot hope to employ them: already an estimated one million Burkinabes work abroad, mostly in the neighbouring Ivory Coast. While the World Bank and IMF talk about structural adjustment programmes, the aid agencies will carry out schemes according to their own priorities: they supply some 15 per cent of the country's GNP at the moment.

But without denying the need for sensible domestic economics or the value of much of the aid work, it all seems desperately precarious. Even assuming that the country has reasonably wise economic policies and that the aid programmes are maintained in real terms – neither of which is a safe assumption – it will be a tremendous struggle.

The question that keeps coming back is: this is a delightful country and under the circumstances they are not managing too badly, but what is the comparative advantage of a small landlocked country on the edge of the Sahara in a harsh competitive world?

- Tourism? It cannot offer golden beaches. There is also an opportunity for cultural tourism – Ouagadougou is home to the Pan-African Film Festival. But tourism requires investment.
- Merchandise exports? Burkina Faso is not going to become a manufacturing centre for electronic goods, following the path of the dynamic East Asian economies.
- Minerals? There are gold, zinc and manganese reserves and some production, but the country is competing against South Africa, which mines on a vastly larger scale. There is no coal, oil of gas, and one of the country's problems is the reliance of the rural population on wood as a fuel for cooking.
- Agricultural exports? Getting the produce exported is the key problem.

All trade links with the rest of the world have to be undertaken through an exchange rate that Burkina Faso does not itself control: the currency is the CFA franc, run by the French for the former West African territories. That is fine if the rate is appropriate; not so good if that rate is wrong.

Given all these difficulties, Burkina Faso has not done too badly: it has managed to increase standards of living through the 1980s, which is more than most of Africa achieved.

It goes almost without saying that granting access to European markets is far more use than any handouts. Viewed from here, Europe appears less than helpful. Before the devaluation of the CFA franc in 1994, subsidised beef from the European Union's beef mountain was being sold here in Ouagadougou, thus undercutting domestic livestock producers.

1. Explain the meaning of Burkina Faso as 'in the UNDP's 1993 Human Development Report is ranked 170 out of 173 countries'. [10 marks]

2. Examine the problems facing Burkina Faso in determining its comparative advantage as 'a small landlocked country on the edge of the Sahara in a harsh competitive world.' [25 marks]

3. Explain how Burkina Faso has encountered difficulties concerning its international trade arising from decisions not made by its government but taken in Western Europe. [15 marks]

Chapter Two

The meaning and measurement of economic development

'Development means modernization, and modernization means transformation of human beings. Development as an objective and development as a process both embrace a change in fundamental attitudes to life and work, and in social, cultural and political institutions.' Paul Streeten

The development process is *multidimensional*. That is, it involves changes over time not only in the economy but also in institutions, political and social structures and cultural values.

Development implies *progress* or *improvement*, which in turn means that we make **value judgements** as to what is deemed desirable or undesirable.

Development is thus a *normative concept* and the definition of development will vary between individuals, political parties and countries. My definition of development may differ from that of others and I may feel that my definition is superior. I cannot prove that superiority, however, I can only assert it – my definition of development is merely different from, not better than, yours.

If we accept that the notion of **economic development** embodies value judgements, it is clear that *economic growth and economic development are not synonymous*. GNP *per capita* might be rising, but at the same time poverty might be increasing, inequality in the distribution of income might be rising and massive environmental damage might be occurring. It would be difficult to describe such a situation as progress! Economic growth might well be a *necessary condition* for economic development but it is not a *sufficient condition*.

The idea that economic growth need not lead to economic development led to a search for a definition of economic development. It was the British economist, Dudley Seers, who posed the question

> *'What are the necessary conditions for a universally accepted aim, the realization of the potential of human personality?'*

Seers argued that if economic growth did *not* lead to a reduction in poverty, inequality and unemployment, then economic development

DEFINITIONS OF DEVELOPMENT

Michael Todaro argues that three basic core values should serve as a conceptual basis and practical guideline for understanding the 'inner meaning' of development. The core values are:

- *sustenance:* the ability to meet basic needs (food, health, shelter and protection);
- *self-esteem:* a sense of worth and self-respect (implying dignity, honour, recognition);
- *freedom:* an expanded range of choices for societies (including freedom from oppression, material wants, greater protection from environmental disasters).

Another notion of development is **sustainable development**. This is defined as *'development that meets the needs of the present without compromising the ability of future generations to meet their own needs'* (World Commission on Environment and Development, 1987). A key element of this notion lies in its emphasis on maintaining **intergenerational welfare** over time – to quote the leading environmental economist, David Pearce, this involves *'providing a bequest to the next generation of an amount and quality of wealth which is at least equal to that inherited by the current generation'*, with wealth defined to include both the human-made and natural stock of assets. These conceptions of development raise enormous political and social issues.

- Are any countries developed on the basis of Todaro's criteria (they may be rich but that is not the same as developed!)?
- Are current models of development sustainable, given the depletion of the Earth's natural wealth and the environmental problems (the depletion of the ozone layer, the destruction of rain forests) that are receiving increasing attention?
- Economics alone cannot provide answers to these questions.

could not be said to be occurring. Development is also increasingly seen to require political democracy and participation, issues which come under the heading of **'good governance'**.

The measurement of *per capita* income

All countries have adopted the conventions (the United Nations' Standard National Accounts) for the calculation of **gross national**

product (GNP) and **gross domestic product** (GDP), and GNP or GDP *per capita* is the commonest indicator of the level of development. 'Economic growth' refers to an increase in either of these indicators. There are, however, well-known problems associated with the calculation of national income in poor countries and its use as an indicator of development:

- The necessary data are often incomplete, unreliable or not available.
- The accounting conventions are not necessarily appropriate; the services of women working in the household are excluded from national income statistics yet in many poor countries, especially in sub-Saharan Africa, women are often responsible for running the family farm as well as working in the household.
- In most poor countries, there is a large subsistence sector – that is, farmers may well consume all or a large proportion of what they produce, rather than sending it to market where it would be counted for the purposes of calculating national income. Statisticians make an allowance for this non-marketed component of output, and for rural capital formation that may not enter the national accounts – housebuilding, irrigation ditches – but it is generally accepted that the value of these activities is underestimated, thus biassing downwards the national income figures for poor countries.
- Income may be overstated for developed economies because a number of items that are included as income might better be seen as costs and hence excluded from income – the cost of travelling to work, for example, or the cost of heating the home in temperate climates.
- *Per capita* (average) incomes tell us nothing about the *distribution of income*. Two countries with similar *per capita* incomes may have very different income distributions, with important implications for the welfare of their populations and the nature and characteristics of the development process. We look at this issue in greater detail in Chapter 5.

Significant problems arise when international comparisons of income levels are made. Income data measured in national currencies have to be converted into a common currency, usually the US dollar, and an exchange rate must thus be chosen. If poor countries artificially maintain overvalued exchange rates (that is, the price of foreign currencies in terms of their domestic currency is too low), this will overstate the income of the country expressed in US dollars.

Offsetting this, however, is the fact that many goods and services in poor countries are not traded and hence have no impact on the exchange rate. Many of the necessities of life in poor countries – basic foodstuffs for example – are very low priced in dollar terms, and a haircut in Kampala, Uganda, will cost less than one in Paris or London.

According to World Bank data:

- Mozambique with an estimated GNP *per capita* of US$60 in 1992 was the poorest country in the world;
- Switzerland, with a GNP *per capita* of US$36 080, was the richest.

Is the average Swiss citizen 600 times better off than the average Mozambican? To put that question slightly differently, does it make sense to state that in Mozambique, on average, people live on 16 cents a day?

Clearly nobody in a developed economy could survive on such a low income. Given that the majority of Mozambicans do survive, it must be the case that the necessities essential for survival cost less in Mozambique than for example in Switzerland, and/or $60 is not a meaningful estimate of *per capita* income in Mozambique. This is not to deny that a huge gap exists between the average incomes of very rich and very poor countries, nor should it lessen our concern with such inequalities. But it does mean that the gap on average is not as great as these statistics would suggest and a number of attempts have been made to compute more meaningful comparisons.

Purchasing power parity comparisons

In order to overcome the problems associated with the use of existing exchange rates, attempts have been made to compare *per capita* incomes of different countries directly by the use of 'international prices'. The theory of **purchasing power parity** (PPP) holds that, in the long run, the exchange rate of two currencies should move towards the rate that would equalize the prices of an identical basket of goods and services in each country. The box gives an example based on the price of a McDonald's Big Mac in a number of countries. Table 2 gives a comparison of GDP *per capita* at local and international prices.

Taking India as an example, we can see that using the conventional measure, India's GDP *per capita* was 1.4 per cent of the US level. Valued at international prices, India's *per capita* income was 5.9 per cent of that of the USA in 1985, still a huge difference and, of course, no less a cause for concern.

13

Big Mac Currencies

Source: *The Economist*, 5 April 1995, p.108

The Big Mac index was devised in 1986 as a light-hearted guide to whether currencies are at a 'correct' level. It is not a precise predictor of currencies, simply a tool to make exchange-rate theory a bit more digestible. Burgernomics is based upon one of the oldest concepts in international economics: the theory of purchasing-power parity (PPP).

Our 'basket' is a McDonald's Big Mac: made to more or less the same recipe in 79 countries. The Big Mac PPP is the exchange rate that would leave hamburgers costing the same in America as abroad. Comparing actual exchange rates with PPP is one indication of whether a currency is under- or overvalued.

The first column of the table shows the local-currency price of a Big Mac; the second shows the dollar one. The cheapest Big Mac is in China: it costs $1.05, compared with an average price in four American cities of $2.32 (all prices include sales tax). At the other extreme, Big Mac munchers in Switzerland pay a beefy $5.20. This is another way of saying that the yuan is the most undervalued currency, the Swiss franc the most overvalued.

The third column calculates Big Mac PPPs (local price divided by price in the USA). For example, dividing the Japanese price by the American one gives a dollar PPP of Y169. On 7 April, the rate was Y84, implying that the yen is 100 per cent overvalued against the dollar — or looking at it from the other point of view, that the dollar is 50 per cent undervalued. On the same basis, the deutschmark is 50 per cent overvalued against its PPP of DM2.07; sterling is 21 per cent overvalued.

The hamburger standard does have its flaws. The theory of PPP relates only to traded goods; the Big Mac is not shipped across borders, and rents (which account for a large share of total costs) vary enormously across countries. Local prices may also be distorted by taxes and trade barriers (e.g. tariffs on beef). Thus while Big Mac PPPs are a handy guide to the cost of living in countries, they may not be a reliable guide to exchange rates.

The Hamburger standard

	Big Mac prices In local currency	In dollars	Implied PPP* of the dollar	Actual $ exchange rate 7/4/95	Local currency under(−)/over (+) valuation†,%
Argentina	Peso3.00	3.00	1.29	1.00	+29
Brazil	Real2.42	2.69	1.04	0.90	+16
Britain	£1.74	2.80	1.33††	1.61††	+21
Chile	Peso950	2.40	409	395	+4
China	Yuan9.00	1.05	3.88	8.54	-55
Germany	DM4.80	3.48	2.07	1.38	+50
Hong Kong	HK$9.50	1.23	4.09	7.73	-47
Indonesia	Rupiah3,900	1.75	1,681	2,231	-25
Japan	Y391	4.65	169	84.2	+100
Malaysia	M$3.76	1.51	1.62	2.49	-35
Mexico	Peso10.9	1.71	4.70	6.37	-26
Singapore	S$2.95	2.10	1.27	1.40	-9
South Korea	Won2,300	2.99	991	769	+29
Taiwan	NT$65.0	2.53	28.0	25.7	+9
Thailand	Baht48.0	1.96	20.7	24.6	-16

*   Purchasing-power parity; local price divided by price in the United States
†   Against dollar
†† Dollars per pound

Table 2 Comparison of national GDP *per capita* at local and international prices, 1985

Country	Valued at local prices		Valued at international prices		Exchange rate* deviation index
	US$	% of US level	US$	% of US level	
	(1)	(2)	(3)	(4)	(5)
Egypt	630	3.8	1,444	9.0	2.4
Ethiopia	100	0.6	390	2.4	4.0
Kenya	246	1.5	727	4.5	3.0
Nigeria	755	4.6	681	4.2	0.9
Zimbabwe	539	3.3	1,216	7.6	2.3
Bangladesh	160	1.0	822	5.1	5.1
India	230	1.4	955	5.9	4.2
Malaysia	2,004	12.2	4,050	25.2	2.1
Pakistan	294	1.8	1,450	9.0	5.0
Sri Lanka	859	5.2	1,995	12.4	2.4
Bolivia	466	2.8	1,328	7.6	2.7
Brazil	1,388	8.4	3,979	24.8	3.0
Colombia	1,211	7.3	3,221	20.1	2.8
Venezuela	2,867	17.4	4,071	25.4	1.5
Australia	10,284	62.4	10,953	68.2	1.1
France	9,245	56.1	12,492	77.8	1.4
Greece	2,944	17.9	5,703	35.5	2.0
United Kingdom	8,041	48.8	10,874	67.7	1.4
USA	16,492	100.0	16,057	100.0	1.0

*Ratio of entries in columns (4) and (1). A value greater than 1 indicates that the local currency is undervalued on a purchasing power parity basis relative to the US dollar.
Source: Colman and Nixson, *Economics of Change in Less Developed Countries,* 3rd edn, Harvester Wheatsheaf, 1994

The Human Development Index (HDI)

The most ambitious attempt to measure development is the **Human Development Index** (HDI). Human development is defined as enlarging peoples' choices. Such choices are, in principle, infinite and change over time, but at all levels of development the three essential ones are:

- for people to live a long and healthy life;
- to acquire knowledge;
- to have access to resources needed for a decent standard of living.

Why do we need a human development index?
Because national progress tends otherwise to be measured by GNP alone, many people have looked for a better, more comprehensive socio-economic measure. The human development index is a contribution to this search.

What does the HDI include?
The HDI is a composite of three basic components of human develop-ment: longevity, knowledge and standard of living. *Longevity* is measured by life expectancy. *Knowledge* is measured by a combination of adult literacy (two-thirds weight) and mean years of schooling (one-third weight). *Standard of living* is measured by purchasing power, based on real GDP per capita adjusted for the local cost of living (purchasing power parity, or PPP).

Why only three components?
The ideal would be to reflect all aspect of human experience. The lack of data imposes some limits on this, and more indicators could perhaps be added as the information becomes available. But more indicators would not necessarily be better. Some might overlap with existing indicators: infant mortality, for example, is already reflected in life expectancy. And adding more variables could confuse the picture and detract from the main trends.

How to combine indicators measured in different units?
The measuring rod for GNP is money. The breakthrough for the HDI, however, was to find a common measuring rod for the socioeconomic distance travelled. The HDI sets a minimum and a maximum for each dimension and then shows where each country stands in relation to these scales – expressed as a value between 0 and 1. So, since the minimum adult literacy rate is 0 per cent and the maximum is 100 per cent, the literacy component of knowledge for a country where the literacy rate if 75 per cent would be 0.75. Similarly, the minimum for life expectancy is 25 years and the maximum 85 years, so the longevity component for a country where life expectancy is 55 years would be 0.5. For income the minimum is \$200 (PPP) and the maximum is \$40,000 (PP). The scores for the three dimensions are then averaged in an overall index.

Is it not misleading to talk of a single HDI for a country with great inequality?
National averages can conceal much. The best solution would be to create separate HDIs for the most significant groups: by gender, for example, or by income group, geographical region, race or ethnic group. Separate HDIs would reveal a more detailed profile of human deprivation in each country, and disaggregated HDIs are already being attempted for countries with sufficient data.

How can the HDI be used?
The HDI offers an alternative to GNP for measuring the relative socio-economic progress of nations. It enables people and their governments to evaluate progress over time and to determine priorities for policy intervention. It also permits instructive comparisons of the experiences in different countries.

Source: UNDP, 1994

The HDI is a composite indicator (see the box on page 16). The HDI has been adjusted by the UNDP to take into account income distribution and **gender inequalities** and it can be disaggregated to take into account **racial inequalities** (South Africa) and regional disparities within countries (Brazil, Nigeria and Egypt, for example).

The HDI ranges between 0 and 1. Table 3 gives the HDI and GNP rankings for a sample of rich and poor countries. It can be seen that

Table 3 HDI ranking for selected industrial and developing countries

	HDI value	HDI rank	GNP per-capita rank	GNP per capita rank minus HDI rank
Canada	0.932	1	11	10
Switzerland	0.931	2	1	−1
Japan	0.929	3	3	0
Sweden	0.928	4	4	0
Norway	0.928	5	5	0
France	0.927	6	13	7
Australia	0.926	7	18	11
USA	0.925	8	9	1
Netherlands	0.923	9	16	7
United Kingdom	0.919	10	19	9
Barbados	0.894	20	34	14
Hong Kong	0.875	24	22	−2
Cyprus	0.873	26	30	4
Korea, Rep. of	0.859	32	36	4
Uruguay	0.859	33	53	20
Trinidad and Tobago	0.855	35	46	11
Bahamas	0.854	36	26	−10
Argentina	0.853	37	43	6
Chile	0.848	38	66	28
Costa Rica	0.848	39	75	36
United Arab Emirates	0.771	62	10	−52
Saudi Arabia	0.742	67	31	−36
Sri Lanka	0.665	90	128	38
Nicaragua	0.583	106	139	33
Vietnam	0.514	116	150	34
Mozambique	0.252	159	173	14
Ethiopia	0.249	161	171	10
Somalia	0.217	165	172	7
Gambia	0.215	166	155	−22
Mali	0.214	167	155	−12
Chad	0.212	168	161	−7
Niger	0.209	169	148	−21
Sierra Leone	0.209	170	163	−7
Afghanistan	0.208	171	169	−2
Guinea	0.191	173	129	−44

Source: UNDP, 1994

Table 4 HDI values by region, 1960–92

	1960	1992	Absolute increase in HDI value 1960–92
All developing countries	0.260	0.541	0.281
Least developed countries	0.165	0.307	0.142
Industrial*	0.799	0.918	0.119
World	0.392	0.605	0.213
Sub-Saharan Africa	0.200	0.357	0.156
Middle East and North Africa	0.277	0.631	0.354
South Asia	0.202	0.376	0.174
East Asia	0.255	0.653	0.397
South-East Asia and Oceania	0.284	0.613	0.329
Latin America and the Caribbean	0.467	0.757	0.290
excl. Mexico and Brazil	0.504	0.735	0.231

*Excluding Eastern Europe and the former Soviet Union
Source: UNDP, 1994

Canada has the highest HDI value but not the highest GNP *per capita*. At the other end of the scale, Mozambique, the poorest country in the world, does not have the lowest HDI value. That dubious distinction goes to Guinea. The final column of Table 3 indicates the discrepancy between the two rankings, and in some cases, these differences are quite large. In the case of Saudi Arabia and the United Arab Emirates, rankings based on GNP *per capita* are significantly above those based on HDI values. In the case of countries like Vietnam, Sri Lanka and Nicaragua, the opposite is the case. These discrepancies in large part reflect the priorities that different countries attach to health and education, especially the education of women.

A comparison of HDIs over time reveals some interesting trends and re-emphasizes the point made above that care needs to be excercised when making statements about the development process and experience. As Table 4 shows, all countries made substantial progress in human development over the period 1960–92. The overall HDI for the least developed countries and those in Sub-Saharan Africa increased by approximately 80 per cent, although they started from very low levels.

In East Africa, the HDI increased two and a half times over the same period, indicating that investment in human development is both a cause and consequence of rapid economic growth. It is interesting to

Table 5 Basic indicators

	Population (millions) mid-1992	GNP per capita, 1992 ($)	Avg. ann. growth (%), 1980–92	Life expectancy at birth (years) 1992	Adult illiteracy (%) Total 1990
Low-income economies excluding China and India					
Mozambique	16.5	60	–3.6	44	67
Ethiopia	54.8	110	–1.9	49	–
Tanzania	25.9	110	0.0	51	–
Sierra Leone	4.4	160	–1.4	43	79
Nepal	19.9	170	2.0	54	74
Bangladesh	114.4	220	1.8	55	65
India	883.6	310	3.1	61	52
China	1,162.2	470	7.6	69	27
Egypt, Arab Rep.	54.7	640	1.8	62	52
Lower-middle income					
Bolivia	7.5	680	–1.5	60	23
Peru	22.4	950	–2.8	65	15
Ecuador	11.0	1,070	–0.3	67	14
Colombia	33.4	1,330	1.4	69	13
Poland	38.4	1,910	0.1	70	–
Turkey	58.5	1,980	2.9	67	19
Russian Federation	149.0	2,510	–	69	–
Upper-middle income					
South Africa	39.8	2,670	0.1	63	–
Brazil	153.9	2,770	0.4	66	19
Hungary	10.3	2,970	0.2	69	–
Greece	10.3	7,290	1.0	77	7
Portugal	9.8	7,450	3.1	74	15
High-income					
Ireland	3.5	12,210	3.4	75	–
New Zealand	3.4	12,300	0.6	76	*
Israel	5.1	13,220	1.9	76	–
Spain	39.1	13,970	2.9	77	5
Hong Kong	5.8	15,360	5.5	78	–
Singapore	2.8	15,730	5.3	75	–
Australia	17.5	17,260	1.6	77	*
United Kingdom	57.8	17,790	2.4	76	*
Italy	57.8	20,460	2.2	77	*
Netherlands	15.2	20,480	1.7	77	*
Canada	27.4	20,710	1.8	78	*
Belgium	10.0	20,880	2.0	76	*
Finland	5.0	21,970	2.0	75	*
United Arab Emirates	1.7	22,020	–4.3	72	*
France	57.4	22,260	1.7	77	*
Austria	7.9	22,380	2.0	77	*
Germany	80.6	23,030	2.4	76	*
United States	255.4	23,240	1.7	77	*
Norway	4.3	25,820	2.2	77	*
Denmark	5.2	26,000	2.1	75	*
Sweden	8.7	27,010	1.5	78	*
Japan	124.5	28,190	3.6	79	*
Switzerland	6.9	36,080	1.4	78	*
World	5,438.2	4,280	1.2	66	35

*According to UNESCO, illiteracy is less than 5 per cent
Source: World Bank, 1994

compare trends in the HDI with trends in *per capita* income. No country experienced a fall in its HDI over the period covered, and the UNDP concludes that '*Human capital, once it is built up, is more likely to be sustainable*'.

Finally, Table 5 gives some basic indicators, including literacy data, for many countries.

Conclusions

The search for a composite indicator of development will continue, even though it is recognized that it is virtually impossible to give every aspect of social progress a money value. Most economists would accept that information on how much is produced (GNP or GDP) must be supplemented by information on what is produced, by what means, for whom and with what impact. What is required, therefore, are indicators of the composition and beneficiaries of GNP/GDP which will supplement, but not replace, GNP/GDP data.

However, not everyone would agree with the notion of development as modernization, and the debate over the meaning of development is likely to be long-running.

KEY WORDS

Value judgements	Gross national product
Economic development	Gross domestic product
Sustainable development	Purchasing power parity
Intergenerational welfare	Human Development Index
Good governance	Gender inequalities
Per capita income	Racial inequalities

Reading list

Maunder, P., *et al.*, Chapter 31 in *Economics Explained*, 3rd edn, Collins Educational, 1995.

Essay topics

1. According to the 1993 *World Development Report*, the GNP *per capita* in Tanzania in 1991 was $100, whereas in the UK it was estimated to have been $16 550. To what extent does it follow that economic welfare in the UK in 1991 was 165 times greater than in Tanzania? [100 marks]

[University of London Examinations and Assessment Council 1996]

2. Explain whether or not you regard economic growth as a desirable objective of economic policy for any government. Compare the obstacles to achieving a satisfactory growth rate in the UK with those in countries such as Ethiopia and Chile. [25 marks]
   [Northern Examinations and Assessment Board 1993]

3. 'Much effort is spent calculating GNP *per capita*, yet many economists would say it is hardly the best measure of the quality of life in a country' (adapted from *The Straits Times*, 25 December 1993). Explain the problems involved in calculating the GNP *per capita* and discuss whether you support its use as a measure of the quality of life in a country. [25 marks]
   [University of Cambridge Local Examinations Syndicate 1995]

4. 'Calculations of Gross National Product (GNP), especially in poor countries, are largely guesswork and, even if they were accurate, the GNP itself can be a very poor measure of welfare'. Discuss this view of the problems of measuring and using GNP statistics.
   [University of Cambridge Local Examinations Syndicate 1992]

Data Response Question

The Human Development Index (HDI)
This task is based on a question set by the University of Cambridge Local Examinations Syndicate in 1996. Study the following information and then answer the questions.

In 1990 the United Nations Development Programme (UNDP) introduced its human development index (HDI) as an alternative measure of economic and social progress, because gross national product (GNP) is a poor measure of relative living standards. The index is a mix of life expectancy, adult literacy, average years of schooling and GNP per head (measured at purchasing-power parity, ppp)*. The table shows indicators and rankings for a selection of developing countries in 1990.

*ppp calculated when the exchange rate reflects domestic purchasing power.

	GNP per head ($)	GNP per head (ppp$)	life expectancy at birth (years)	adult literacy (%)	GNP per head ($)	HDI
Mozambique	80	620	47	39	125th	112th
Ethiopia	110	310	42	66	122nd	106th
Uganda	220	800	52	58	112th	121st
Nigeria	290	1420	51	43	108th	101st
India	350	1150	59	43	104th	88th
Indonesia	570	2350	57	74	90th	71st
Phillipines	730	2320	64	86	78th	59th

© *Human Development Report 1992,* adapted by permission of the UNDP

1. (a) How does the world ranking of these developing countries change if it is measured by the human development index (HDI) rather than GNP per head ($)? [2 marks]
   (b) Explain *two* reasons why GNP is a poor measure of relative living standards. [4 marks]
2. Further indicators might be included in the human development index to make it an even better measure of a country's standard of living. Suggest *two* further indicators which you might use and explain your choice. [4 marks]
3. (a) Explain the relationship you would expect to find between the level of adult literacy and GNP per head ($). [2 marks]
   (b) To what extent does the data on adult literacy and GNP per head ($) confirm this relationship? [2 marks]
4. Economic development often produces a change in average life expectancy and the age distribution of the population. Discuss how this might affect average living standards. [6 marks]

Chapter Three

Development theory

'If development economics is to have credibility, there must be a commonality among the countries it studies, a unity in diversity.'
Barbara Ingham, University of Salford

Characteristics of less-developed countries

As we have seen, the notion of a 'Third World' is based on the presumption that poor, less-developed countries (LDCs) share a set of common economic, social, political and institutional characteristics. By 'adding up' such characteristics, some economists have attempted to explain the origins of poverty and its persistence over time.

In one of the most widely used textbooks (Michael Todaro, *Economic Development*, 5th edn, Longman, 1994) the common characteristics of LDCs are listed thus:

- low levels of living, comprising low incomes, high inequality, poor health and inadequate education;
- low levels of productivity;
- high rates of population growth and dependency burdens;
- significant dependence on agricultural production and primary product exports;
- dominance, dependence and vulnerability in international relations.

At the same time, there is great diversity both within and between LDCs, with respect to both their historical experiences and their contemporary economic performance. For example, while it is true that the great majority of poor countries were at one time colonies of the metropolitan powers (Spain, Portugal, Netherlands, France, Belgium, the UK and, at a later stage, Japan), the impact and consequences of colonial rule varied widely between countries and over time.

More recently, most poor countries have attempted to industrialize. Some have achieved great success in the endeavour (the economies of East and South East Asia), while others (the majority of the economies of Sub-Saharan Africa) have not yet succeeded. As the data in Table 5 showed, there are huge differences in geographical area and population size, and increasingly – given the differences in rates of economic growth between countries – in *per capita* incomes.

Differences in resource endowments also exist, with some of the poorest countries (Zaire and Angola, for example) having great natural resource endowments.

Given the diversity of experience, endowment and performance, we must be careful not to oversimplify theories and explanations of under-development and development. Of necessity, economists have to simplify and generalize in order to construct theories which give them testable hypotheses. But we must not lose sight of the historical and global dimensions of development, and the need for new – and perhaps unorthodox – explanations for the persistence of poverty and inequality.

Introduction to the theory

The theoretical origins of development economics as a sub-discipline are remarkably diverse. They were:

- the 'Keynesian revolution', with its justification of government intervention in order to achieve macroeconomic targets;
- early growth theory, especially the **Harrod–Domar model** (see below);
- the experience of wartime planning and intervention in the economy in the UK and the USA;
- the example of the Soviet Union's rapid industrialization in the 1930s;
- decolonization – the concern with economic development of political parties campaigning for independence in the colonies and planning by governments in newly independent states (India, for example).

This diversity of theoretical inputs, historical experience and political expediency has meant that development economists, while using the tools of orthodox economic analysis, have nevertheless often been highly unorthodox in their approach to development problems. Nevertheless, most have shared a number of common concerns.

- Attention has been focused on the long-run, with economic growth usually taking priority over considerations of static **allocative efficiency**.
- Economic growth and changes in the structure of output, employment and consumption, and patterns of trade, have been closely linked to one another.
- The focus has been on savings and investment (**accumulation**) and the policies and institutions required to encourage and sustain the accumulation process.

- The development of human resources, through expenditure on health and education, has always been seen as an important aspect of the development process (**human capital formation**).
- Alternative development strategies – some highly unorthodox – have been given serious consideration and have often influenced the policy-making process.

Alternative theoretical perspectives on development

Development economists have perhaps been more prepared than others to recognize the need for, and the existence of, a variety of theoretical approaches to the study of economic development. Economists discussing development therefore consider differing questions, and as a result come up with differing answers and – most importantly – differing policy recommendations. For the sake of simplicity, we can identify three schools of thought: orthodox, structuralist and radical.

● The orthodox school

The orthodox (sometimes referred to as **neoclassical**) school focuses attention on the *efficiency* with which resources are allocated. Unnecessary government intervention in product and factor markets gives rise to 'distorted' relative prices, because (i) limits on interest rates make capital too 'cheap', (ii) minimum-wage legislation raises wages above their market clearing level, and (iii) tariffs imposed on imported commodities raise domestic prices above international prices. This in turn gives rise to a misallocation of resources because industry is overprotected, relative to agriculture for example.

The World Bank's recommendation that countries should 'get prices right' illustrates the view that markets lead to the most efficient resource allocation, and that government intervention should be confined to the provision of macroeconomic stability, security to the owners of property, and any action necessary to overcome market failures. World Bank policies in the 1980s illustrate the application of orthodox macro- and microeconomic policies.

● The structuralist school

The **structuralist** school of thought emerged largely in Latin America after the Second World War, principally as a reaction to what were seen as irrelevant orthodox theories.

Structuralists argued that LDCs were characterized by a variety of constraints, which meant that either markets did not exist or that markets operated imperfectly – with outcomes considered undesirable.

25

For example, it was argued that the growth of incomes and urbanization would lead to an increase in demand for foodstuffs. This increase in demand, however, would not stimulate an increase in supply because of the structure of land ownership in the agricultural sector. The large estates (the *latifundia*) would not respond to higher prices because they were not profit-maximizers – land was held for social and political reasons as well as for economic ones. On the other hand the small landowners – the *minifundia* – were at the margins of subsistence and would not be able to take the risk of supplying the market for fear of jeopardizing their own survival. Land ownership was thus a **structural bottleneck**.

Other structuralist theories include the centre–periphery model and the secular deterioration in the terms of trade of primary product exporters (see Chapter 8), and the theory of import substituting industrialization (see Chapter 7).

● **The radical school**
The **radical** school of thought is less easy to characterize. Some economists have argued that poor countries will never develop as long as they remain a part of the global capitalist economy ('the development of underdevelopment', a slogan associated with the American economist Andre Gunder Frank).

Others – for example Fernando Henrique Cardoso, a leading Brazilian sociologist, now President of Brazil – have argued that only 'dependent development' is possible, because of the subordinate position of poor countries in the global economy and the absence of key sectors in those economies (especially the low level of development of the machine-making sector – capital goods).

Yet others take the famous Marxist dictum: '*The country that is more developed industrially only shows to the less developed the image of its own future*'. They argue that capitalist development is occurring on a large scale in many areas of the Third World – as in East and South East Asia, and in parts of Latin America – and that what is needed is a strong government that is able to intervene on a selective basis in the economy in order to promote capital accumulation, both physical and human, and industrialization.

Balanced versus unbalanced growth
The theory of **balanced growth** was the outcome of the work of a number of different economists, and had its origins in the poorer peripheral economies of Eastern and South Eastern Europe in 1943.

Industrialization in that region was constrained by the small size of the domestic market, by the inability of firms to internalize the value of *external economies* that they generated – for example, the training of labour which might then leave to work for other firms – and by the inability of firms to anticipate the external economies generated by the investment of other firms.

If a number of consumer goods industries were established simultaneously, the workers in one factory would provide the market for the output of other factories. This was the idea behind the 'Big Push' theory of industrialization. It highlighted the need for state intervention – to invest in training the labour force, to plan and organize the large-scale investment programme, and to help mobilize the necessary finance. Balanced growth thus became associated with 'planning' and industrialization.

It quickly became apparent that a strategy of balanced growth was beyond the resources of most poor countries. First, both governments and domestic entrepreneurs would have to provide the impetus to growth. Secondly, the scale of the resource mobilization effort would have to be huge. Thirdly, the investment programme itself would have to be sufficiently large to overcome the diseconomies of small scale, to reduce the risks of market failure and to exploit external economies fully.

Critics of balanced growth thus argued that LDCs had neither the organizational nor the managerial skills to implement such a strategy and that **unbalanced growth** was more practicable.

Planners and policy-makers would no longer attempt to anticipate supply and demand imbalances but would allow the market to reveal bottlenecks. The latter would then *induce* investment, from both the public and private sector, to overcome them. The American economist Albert Hirschman, in particular, argued that governments should encourage investment in branches of production with significant **inter-industry linkages** – *backward* linkages to raw materials and input supplies, and *forward* linkages with users of the industry's output.

Rostow's stages of economic growth

In 1960, the American economist W.W. Rostow published a book entitled *The Stages of Growth: A Non-Communist Manifesto*. In it he argued that all countries experienced a similar sequence of development, and that countries differed with respect to the stage they were at at any point in time. The five stages he suggested were:

1 the traditional society
2 the transitional stage (the preconditions for takeoff)

3 the takeoff
4 the drive to maturity
5 the stage of high mass consumption.

The rich industrialized market economies were in stages 4 and 5 while the poor countries were seen as being in stages 1 and 2. The latter, transitional stage, was a crucial one, during which there would occur changes in agriculture, transport and international trade, and entrepreneurs would emerge. This stage would be followed by the **takeoff period**, of perhaps ten to twenty years, during which rates of investment would double, leading economic sectors emerge and self-sustaining growth provide for the transition to stages 4 and 5.

The notion of a 'takeoff period' was influential, but the stages theory has been subject to a number of criticisms:

- It is difficult to distinguish between the end of one stage and the beginning of the next.
- The stage of high mass consumption is not the 'end' of development – rich countries undergo structural change (deindustrialization), booms and slumps, and they differ among themselves (compare the UK and Japan).
- The notion of a traditional society, unchanging and common to all poor countries, is not valid.
- The condition of today's poor countries is different from that of the now-rich countries when they were at comparable levels of GNP *per capita*.

Logically, no country can replicate the development experience of another country, as the development of one country changes the economic environment within which other countries develop.

The Harrod–Domar model

Neither of the authors credited with the development of this model was concerned with developing countries, but it has been widely used by economic planners in the Third World.

Once a planner has a rough idea as to how many units of capital are required to produce one unit of output (the *incremental* **capital–output ratio, k**), and the *savings ratio* is known, then the rate of growth of income can be calculated. Alternatively, if a target rate of growth (g) is set, then the required savings ratio (s) can be estimated for any given k.

If it is assumed that *employment* growth is related in some predictable way to *output* growth, this model also gives employment predictions or indicates the rates of growth that must be attained in order to reach employment targets.

THE HARROD-DOMAR MODEL

This model highlights the importance of **capital** accumulation in the theory of economic growth.

In a companion volume in this series, *Supply side economics*, the authors, Healey & Cook, write:

'... *the basic determinants of economic growth are not in dispute. Increase in the labour supply, training and education, investment in physical capital and R&D are unambiguously the prerequisites of supply side success.*'

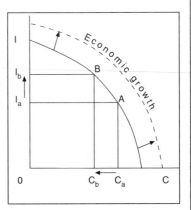

The accompanying production possibility curve summarizes the importance of capital growth. I is the *change* in the capital stock, K. The national income, Y, increases if consumption, C, is reduced, in the short run, from C_a to C_b, to release saving, S, and resources for additional I, from I_a to I_b.

In the long run, the increase in the economy's capacity shifts the production possibility frontier outwards to the pecked line which can then allow both higher C and higher I. Journalists refer to this process as '*less jam today, more jam tomorrow*'.

The Harrod-Domar model assumes a fixed relationship between capital stock, K and output, Y. This is expressed as a capital-output ratio.

To continue the rest of the Healey/Cook quotation: '*But where economists have failed to provide a clear lead is identifying the factors that influence each of these driving forces that underpin economic growth.*

The Harrod-Domar model is a contribution to this debate.

However, a number of criticisms can be made of the model:

- Is it the level of savings which restricts investment, or is it the lack of profitable investment opportunities that restricts savings?
- The original model assumes a **closed economy**, but once foreign trade is introduced the major constraint on economic growth might well be the availability of foreign exchange rather than domestic savings.
- Is the capital–output ratio fixed? Neoclassical economists will argue that capital and labour will be substituted for one another depending on their relative prices, hence influencing k.

- k will vary between different sectors of the economy (it may be lower in agriculture, for example, than in industry) and thus growth will in part be determined by the distribution of investment between sectors.

Planning and markets

Over the past two decades, ideas on economic policies for development have changed dramatically.

- First, the results of attempts at economic planning have in general been disappointing. The collapse of the previously planned economies of Eastern and Central Europe and the former Soviet Union has further discredited the notion that resources can be more efficiently allocated by the state than by markets.
- Public sectors have been overexpanded. In many countries this has led to the creation of overstaffed, inefficient, loss-making enterprises.
- Governments have allowed public spending to exceed revenue, leading to excessive borrowing, increases in money supply and aggravation of inflationary pressures.

The 1980s saw a change in emphasis in development policy, with the following coming to the top of the agenda:

- **liberalization**, especially of trade;
- **structural adjustment**;
- **privatization**.

A more limited role for government was envisaged focusing on:

- the proper macroeconomic management of the economy;
- the creation of an efficient regulatory and promotional framework;
- investment in education and health (human capital) and **infrastructure** (physical capital);
- protection of poor and vulnerable members of society.

Conclusions

Most development economists would now accept that governments must try to create a 'market-friendly' environment in order to encourage economic development. The recognition that poor countries share common characteristics and face similar problems gives a 'unity in diversity' to the study of development problems. This should not, however, obscure their diversity and the need to design policies that reflect the often unique characteristics of individual countries.

```
┌─────────────────────────────────────────────────────────┐
│                    KEY WORDS                              │
│                                                           │
│  Keynesian revolution         Unbalanced growth          │
│  Harrod–Domar model           Inter-industry links       │
│  Allocative efficiency        Capital–output ratio       │
│  Accumulation                 Capital                     │
│  Human capital formation      Takeoff period             │
│  Neoclassical                 Closed economy             │
│  Structuralist                Liberalization             │
│  Structural bottleneck        Structural adjustment      │
│  Radical                      Privatization              │
│  Dependent development        Infrastructure             │
│  Balanced growth                                          │
│                                                           │
└─────────────────────────────────────────────────────────┘
```

Reading list

Anderton, A., Units 105–108 in *Economics*, Causeway Press, 2nd edn, 1995.

Healey, N., and Cook, M., Chapter 2 in *Supply Side Economics*, 3rd edn, Heinemann Educational, 1996.

Maunder P., *et al.*, Chapter 31 in *Economics Explained*, Collins Educational, 3rd edn, 1995.

Essay topics

1. In 1992, the growth rate of the Singapore economy was over 11 per cent – in the UK, the equivalent rate was just 2 per cent. Suggest some likely reasons for this difference and comment upon its economic implications. [20 marks]
   [University of Cambridge Local Examinations Syndicate, AS level, 1995]

2. (a) Describe the essential characteristics of developing countries. [12 marks]
   (b) Assess the range of policies that a country could pursue to promote its economic development. [13 marks]
   [University of Cambridge Local Examinations Syndicate 1995]

Chapter Four

The global economy and the Third World

'Third World countries were subjected to a series of historically unprecedented external shocks at the beginning of the 1980s ... a number of these adverse factors continued to operate throughout the decade (and into the 1990s) which has made full economic recovery in a large number of developing economies extremely difficult.'
Ajit Singh

There are huge inequalities in the global distribution of income and they are increasing all the time. Between 1960 and 1991, the share of world income for the richest fifth of the global population rose from 70 per cent to 85 per cent. The share of the poorest fifth declined over the same period from 2.3 per cent to 1.4 per cent. There were similar disparities with respect to trade, investment, savings and commercial lending (see Figure 1).

The small economic size and limited economic influence of most poor countries means that they are highly vulnerable to developments within the global economy which are beyond their control but which may have an adverse impact on their income, employment and prospects for economic growth.

The past two decades have been characterized by instability in the global economy.

- The early to mid 1970s witnessed the breakdown of the post-war system of fixed exchange rates (the Bretton Woods system), followed by two oil price shocks (1974/75 and 1979/80) and inflation and recession.

- The 1980s were characterized by slow economic growth, continued economic instability and growing disparities in economic performance between countries. The decade ended with the 'revolutions' in Eastern and Central Europe in 1989, and in 1990 there was the dissolution of the Council for Mutual Economic Assistance (the CMEA or COMECON which was the 'common market' between the Soviet Union and its Eastern and Central European allies).

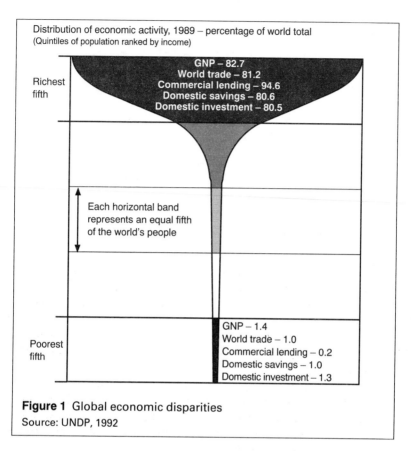

Distribution of economic activity, 1989 – percentage of world total
(Quintiles of population ranked by income)

GNP – 82.7
World trade – 81.2
Commercial lending – 94.6
Domestic savings – 80.6
Domestic investment – 80.5

Richest fifth

Each horizontal band represents an equal fifth of the world's people

Poorest fifth

GNP – 1.4
World trade – 1.0
Commercial lending – 0.2
Domestic savings – 1.0
Domestic investment – 1.3

Figure 1 Global economic disparities
Source: UNDP, 1992

The 1980s was a decade of crisis for the developing countries as a whole, and the period is often referred to as the 'lost decade'. It was subjected to a series of major **external shocks** (see the box on page 34) in the early 1980s, and the continuation of adverse factors throughout the period made economic recovery difficult for many countries. Table 6 gives details of the growth performance of low- and middle-income economies for the period 1982–93.

The aggregate data are somewhat distorted by the inclusion of the 'Europe and Central Asia' group of countries, many of which experienced massive falls in income in the 1991–93 period. Sub-Saharan Africa has also experienced falling incomes *per capita* over the 1982–93 period, as has the Middle East and North Africa group of countries.

Excluding the transitional economies, however, there has been an improvement in the growth performance of poor countries in the

Table 6 Low- and middle-income economies: growth of GDP and GDP *per capita*, 1982–93 (average annual percentage changes)

Region or income group	GDP		GDP per capita	
	1982–90	1991–93	1982–90	1991–93
Low- and middle-income economies	3.4	0.7	1.4	−1.1
By regional group				
Sub-Saharan Africa	2.4	1.4	−0.7	−1.3
East Asia and Pacific	8.1	8.5	6.4	6.9
South Asia	5.7	4.0	3.4	1.5
Middle East and North Africa	0.0	2.7	−3.1	−0.3
Europe and Central Asia	1.9	−10.0	1.1	−10.6
Latin America and the Caribbean	2.3	3.1	0.3	1.2
By income group				
Low- and middle-income economies, excluding transitional economies in Europe and Central Asia	3.8	4.5	1.7	2.5

Source: World Bank, 1994

WHAT ARE EXTERNAL SHOCKS?

The external shocks that most affected the developing countries were largely caused by the slowdown in global economic activity, *especially in the early 1980s*, which affected economic and industrial development through a number of channels:

- a reduction in demand for the developing countries' commodity and mineral *exports*;
- as a consequence, a fall in commodity *prices* and a reduction in the net barter *terms of trade* (see Chapter 7);
- a significant rise in global real *interest rates*, leading to an increase in the real burden of interest and debt repayments of poor debtor countries (see Chapter 10);
- a fall in the quantity of official development assistance (aid) and other *capital flows* to developing countries, resulting in negative net transfer of resources in 1984 and subsequent years for Latin America and Africa.

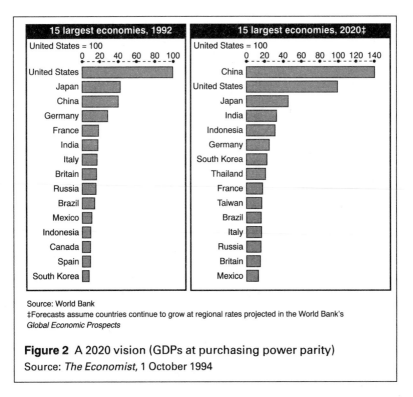

Source: World Bank
‡Forecasts assume countries continue to grow at regional rates projected in the World Bank's
Global Economic Prospects

Figure 2 A 2020 vision (GDPs at purchasing power parity)
Source: *The Economist*, 1 October 1994

1990s, largely the result of the rapid growth of the East Asia and Pacific group of countries. This region includes the original 'Gang of Four' – Singapore, Hong Kong, Taiwan (not included in Table 6) and South Korea – as well as a number of other rapidly growing **Newly Industrializing Economies**, or NIEs: Malaysia, Thailand, Indonesia and China.

China has been the fastest growing economy in the world for most of the 1980s and 90s. According to some forecasts (see Figure 2), taking crude extrapolations of current growth rates, the Chinese economy will be 40 per cent larger (in absolute terms) than that of the USA by the year 2020, with the developing countries (including Eastern Europe and the former Soviet Union) accounting for over 60 per cent of world output.

Development economists quite properly continue to focus attention on issues of global poverty, inequality and instability. The western media often presents an image of the Third World that reinforces popular notions of *famine and crisis*. There is, however, great diversity within the 'developing world' with respect to history, political evolution, institutions, and growth and development performance. It would be misleading to ignore the profound changes that are occurring in the global economy.

Conclusions

The small *economic* size of the majority of poor countries makes them extremely vulnerable to adverse changes in global economic conditions. Some economies have been able to adjust to changed circumstances and have sustained long periods of rapid economic growth. Others have been unable to adjust and face economic stagnation and social and political crisis.

Economists disagree as to what factors determine a country's ability to adjust. Orthodox economists emphasize the importance of *free trade* and *the market* in reallocating resources and making an economy open to competitive pressures. Others point to the role of the 'developmental state' in the East Asian context (see Chapter 7) and emphasize the importance of selective intervention by governments to ensure the achievement of development objectives.

KEY WORDS

External shocks   Developmental state
Newly Industrializing
   Economies

Essay topics

1. What are the fundamental characteristics of the world's less developed economies? Evaluate debt relief, international loans and stabilizing the demand for and price of primary commodities, as means of stimulating the economic development of these economies. [25 marks]
   [Northern Examinations and Assessment Board 1994]
2. (a) Explain how less developed economies are dependent on developed countries for their economic well-being. [12 marks]
   (b) To what extent is this dependency the main problem facing the less developed economies? [8 marks]
   [University of Cambridge Local Examinations Syndicate, AS level, 1993]

Data Response Question

This task is based on a question set in a specimen paper by the University of London Examinations and Assessment Council. Read the article entitled 'Brave new world of services exports is folly', by R. Rowthorn, which appeared in the *Guardian* on 30 May 1994. Then answer the questions.

Over the past 20 years, industrial employment has either stagnated or fallen in almost every advanced economy. Meanwhile, the service sector has grown dramatically and now accounts for about two-thirds of all jobs in the Organisation for Economic Co-operation and Development (OECD). Some view these developments as a sign of economic decline. Other see them as the dawn of a post-industrial age in which manufacturing industry will no longer be crucial to the prosperity of rich countries, whose economies will be devoted almost exclusively to services. Those who take this latter view expect rich countries to buy those manufactured goods they need from poorer industrialising countries. In return, rich countries will offer services, such as banking and consultancy. Manufacturing industry migrates to the developing countries, while advanced countries specialise in services. However, the chart, which shows what has happened to manufacturing trade between advanced and developing countries over the past 25 years, portrays a rather different picture.

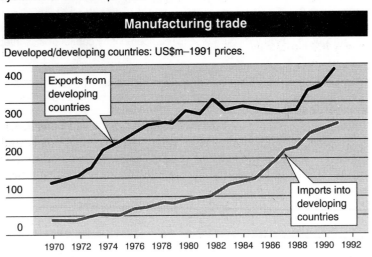

Manufacturing trade

Developed/developing countries: US$m–1991 prices.

Exports from developing countries

Imports into developing countries

Source: *UN/John Wells*

Following the oil and commodity price increases around 1973, there was a massive surge of exports of capital and intermediate goods from the advanced countries to the developing world. This export boom came to an end in the early 1980s as oil prices fell and the debt crisis hit Africa and Latin America. Over the last few years, as capital lending to the developing countries has recovered, there has been a new surge of exports from advanced countries. The share of services in the total exports of advanced countries has remained virtually stationary for 25 years – at about 23 per cent. The share of services in UK exports has actually fallen over this period, reflecting the decline of our shipping fleet and the rise of other service exporters abroad.

Over the same period, exports of financial and other services – which includes all services other than transport and travel – have been growing somewhat faster than those of manufactures. However, the combined revenue from all exports in this category is still very small, being a mere one-tenth of that from manufactures. For the foreseeable future the advanced countries will continue to export manufactured goods on a very large scale to the developing world.

There has been a major shift in the international division of labour but this shift is not from manufacturing to services, but is a shift within the manufacturing sector itself. Many labour-intensive manufacturing activities in the rich countries, such as clothing or assembly, have been put out of business by rising imports from the developing countries, causing jobs to be lost. These manufactured imports have not been financed by the export of services but by the export of other manufactures, especially capital goods and intermediate products such as chemicals. The result is an **emerging new international division of labour.** Adrian Wood of the Institute for Development Studies at Sussex argues that the migration of labour-intensive production to developing countries has destroyed a large number of unskilled jobs in advanced countries. Its replacement by capital or skill-intensive types of manufacturing production has only partly offset the number of jobs lost in labour-intensive activities. The challenge facing the existing advanced economies comes not only from the labour-intensive manufactures imported from much poorer countries but also competition they face from the NICs of Asia and Latin America. They pose a threat right across the board to the established economic leaders, both in advanced manufacturing and services. Singapore, for example, has a trade surplus in services approaching that of Britain; Hong Kong is a major world financial centre; South Korea exports more services than Australia.

1. How might the changes in patterns of employment in OECD countries be explained? [15 marks]
2. Analyse the factors contributing to changes in the trade in manufactured goods between developed and developing countries. [20 marks]
3. Examine the likely economic effects of the 'emerging new international division of labour'. [15 marks]

Chapter Five

Income distribution and development

'Despite its financial crisis, Mexico has achieved one economic distinction: it has the world's fastest growing number of billionaires, with 13 in 1994. The combined wealth of these individuals is more than double the combined wealth of the poorest 17 million Mexicans, whose share of national income is falling.' Oxfam, 1995

In Chapter 1 the focus of attention was on **absolute poverty**. In this chapter we shall be looking at the distribution of income within individual less-developed countries, and emphasizing the notion of **relative poverty** and inequality. The argument here is that poverty must be defined with respect to a **comparator group**.

An individual or a household may have more than enough income to sustain life, but the standard of living may still be very low compared with the average for the country as a whole, and that individual or household would thus still be regarded as 'poor'. As an economy grows – that is, as *per capita* incomes rise – so the income level defining poverty also rises. Relative poverty is thus specific with respect both to time and place.

The majority of poor countries are characterized by a variety of wide economic and social inequalities: inequalities in the distribution of

---

POVERTY AS DEPRIVATION

'Poverty can be defined objectively and applied consistently only in terms of the concept of relative deprivation ... . The term is understood objectively rather than subjectively. Individuals, families and groups in the population can be said to be in poverty when they lack the resources to obtain the types of diets, participate in the activities and have the living conditions and amenities which are customary, or are at least widely encouraged or approved, in the societies to which they belong. Their resources are so seriously below those commanded by the average individual or family that they are, in effect, excluded from ordinary living patterns, customs and activities.' Peter Townsend, 1974

income and wealth; between urban and rural areas; and between different regions and ethnic or racial groups. Inequalities with respect to 'modern' sector facilities (employment, housing, education, health) are also significant.

Economists have focused their attention on the distribution of income, largely because even though the data are often incomplete and inaccurate, they are nevertheless available and are an indication of the wider inequalities referred to above.

The **size distribution of income** shows how many persons or households receive how much income, summarized in the **Lorenz curve** (Figure 3). The 45-degree line, OD, is the line of perfect equality, and the further away the actual Lorenz curve is from the 45-degree line, the greater is the degree of inequality in the size distribution of income. Hence the 'mixed economy' case ($M_1M_2M_3$) is less unequal than the 'Laissez faire' case ($L_1L_2L_3$) in the diagram.

Table 7 shows the income share of the lowest 40 per cent of households for a number of countries. Brazil has the greatest degree of

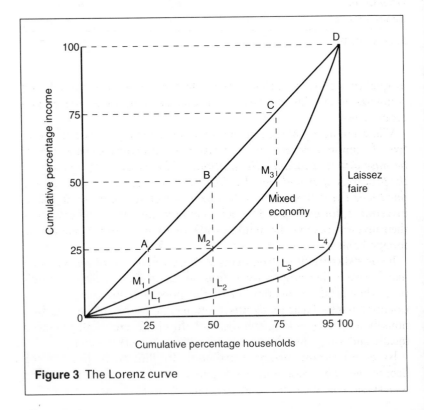

Figure 3 The Lorenz curve

Table 7 Income shares for selected LDCs (countries are ranked according to their HDI)

Country	Income share of lowest 40 per cent of households (per cent) 1980–88
Hong Kong	16.2
Singapore	15.0
Costa Rica	11.6
Malaysia	13.9
Colombia	12.7
Brazil	8.1
Jamaica	15.3
Philippines	15.2
Peru	12.9
Indonesia	21.2
Pakistan	19.0
India	20.4
Ivory Coast	13.0
Bangladesh	23.7

Source: UNDP, 1992

inequality according to this measure. In general, poor less-developed countries have higher levels of inequality than richer developed economies.

While a more equitable distribution of income may well be an objective of economic development, it also has a **functional value**. *This is because different income distributions will have varying impacts on the processes of growth and development in any given economy at any one time.* The distribution of income may well influence savings and investment, for example. The rich may save more than the poor, but their investments may be in non-productive assets – urban real estate, foreign bank accounts, etc.

Income distribution also affects *patterns of consumption*. The rich may have a higher propensity to consume luxury, imported commodities, whereas the consumption of the poor will be dominated by essential items – basic foodstuffs, clothing and footwear, housing and household items (cooking utensils, basic furniture, etc.) – all produced locally and using unsophisticated, labour-intensive technologies.

Issues concerning income distribution are thus at the heart of the debate over *what* economic development should be about (**normative** issues) and *how* it can be achieved (**policy** issues).

Conclusions

Many economists argue that there is a conflict between **equity** and **efficiency**. This means that economies that emphasize greater equality – through, for example, land reform, highly progressive taxation and an interventionist state – may as a result sacrifice economic growth. Put the other way round, *economies that wish to grow rapidly must accept greater inequality in the distribution of income*. Greater equality is thus seen as a 'luxury' that poor countries cannot afford, but which may be attainable once higher *per capita* incomes are achieved.

Economists have looked long and hard at the data on economic growth and income distribution. Most have concluded that there is no hard and fast relationship. The East Asian economies have grown rapidly with below-average levels of inequality (this is especially true of Taiwan – see Figure 4). Other economies emphasizing greater equality – for example Cuba – are experiencing severe economic difficulties, not least owing to the lack of material incentives and inadequate market mechanisms. China is now a rapidly growing

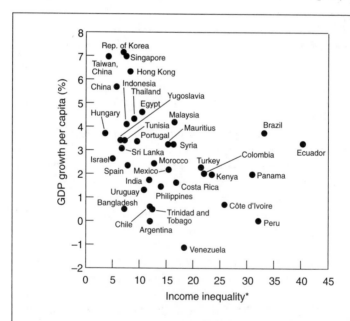

Figure 4 Income inequality* and the growth of GDP, 1965–89

* The ratio of the income shares of the richest 20 per cent and poorest 20 per cent of the population. Data on income distribution are from surveys conducted mainly in the late 1960s and early 70s. Source: World Bank, 1991

economy and inequality is undoubtedly on the increase. Many Sub-Saharan African economies are highly unequal and stagnant.

There is thus no simple economic model linking growth and equity. Inequality and poverty together condemn large numbers of people to malnutrition, poor housing, limited educational opportunities and unemployment. A redistribution of income could raise the productivity and hence the output of such people by making them healthier, better educated and more active participants in the development process.

Progressive taxation might also curb excessive **conspicuous consumption** by the rich in poor countries, thus increasing saving and, it is hoped, productive investment.

KEY WORDS

Absolute poverty   Normative
Relative poverty   Policy
Comparator group   Equity
Size distribution of income   Efficiency
Lorenz curve   Conspicuous consumption
Functional value

Reading list

Wilkinson, M., *Equity, Efficiency and Market Failure*, 2nd edn, Heinmann Educational, 1996.

Chapter Six

Population and environment

'*Population must not be treated as an optional extra when concerns of poverty alleviation and sustainable development are being negotiated. We need a truly integrated set of population, environment and development policies.*' Dr Nafis Sadik, Secretary General of the International Conference on Population and Development, Cairo, 1994

The second half of the twentieth century has witnessed a population explosion. From 1900 to 1950, the world's human population is estimated to have grown from 1.6 to 2.5 billion people. By the year 2000 it will probably have exceeded 6 billion people, 4.8 billion of whom will live in poor countries. Hence the century will have experienced an approximately four-fold population increase, with the post-1950 period more than doubling the figure.

The main factor responsible for the increase has been the rapid increase in **population growth** in developing countries. Growth peaked at 2.5 per cent a year around 1970 and has subsequently slowly declined to just under 2 per cent. In the industrialized countries, the rate of growth of population in 1990 was 0.6 per cent a year.

Future growth of the global population is built into its present age structure. A very high proportion of the populations of developing countries is young. For example, in 1990, 45 per cent of the population of Africa and 37 per cent of the population of Latin America and South Asia were below the age of 15 (compared with 22 per cent for the industrialized economies). Whatever happens to female **fertility** – that is, the number of children women have – huge future increases in population can be expected.

Current estimates put global population in the middle of the twenty-first century at anywhere between 7.1 billion and 11.9 billion people. Clearly poor countries will face massive problems in terms of employment, industrialization, technology choice and the environment in dealing with such increased numbers of people.

Population growth is caused by **birth rates** exceeding **death rates**. In LDCs, death rates have fallen more rapidly than birth rates, while the opposite has occurred in the developed economies. Death rates fall as a result of improvements in nutrition and material conditions and the spread of medical knowledge and treatment. Reduced **infant mortality** and increased longevity for those who survive childhood have contributed to the decline in the death rate, and this in turn is reflected in increased **life expectancy.**

A decline in death rates (especially infant mortality rates) is followed, with a lag, by a fall in birth rates. Almost all studies of the determinants of fertility indicate that as fewer babies under the age of one year die, this leads to a fall, with a lag, in the birth rate. Other determinants of fertility include female education, labour-force participation, the availability of family planning services, and the effects of improved economic well-being. The fall in birth rates following the fall in death rates is known as the **demographic transition.**

Country variations in population growth and total fertility rates are given in Table 8. Some countries have dramatically reduced population

Table 8 Population growth and total fertility rates in selected LDCs

	1992 population estimate (millions)	Average annual growth of population (%)			Total fertility rate	
		1970–80	1980–92	1992–2000	1970	1992
China	1162	1.8	1.4	1.0	5.8	2.0
India	884	2.3	2.1	1.7	5.8	3.7
Bangladesh	114	2.6	2.3	1.8	7.0	4.0
Pakistan	119	3.1	3.1	2.7	7.0	5.6
Sri Lanka	17	1.6	1.4	1.1	4.3	2.5
Indonesia	184	2.3	1.8	1.4	5.5	2.9
Malaysia	19	2.4	2.5	2.0	5.5	3.5
Philippines	64	2.5	2.4	2.3	6.4	4.1
Korea, Republic of	44	1.8	1.1	0.8	4.3	1.8
Singapore	3	2.0	1.8	1.4	3.1	1.8
Brazil	154	2.4	2.0	1.4	4.9	2.8
Mexico	85	2.9	2.0	1.9	6.5	3.2
Egypt	55	2.1	2.4	1.7	5.9	3.8
Nigeria	102	2.9	3.0	2.8	6.9	5.9
Kenya	26	3.7	3.6	2.5	8.0	5.4

Note: Total fertility rate represents the number of children that would be born to a woman if she were to live to the end of her childbearing years and bear children at each age in accordance with prevailing age-specific fertility rates.

Source: World Bank, 1994

growth and fertility rates – China, Korea and Singapore for example – while others have made less progress. Pakistan, Kenya and Nigeria have high population growth rates and fertility rates.

Economic consequences of population growth

Rapid population growth has a number of economic consequences:

- A high proportion of the population is aged 15 and under, increasing pressure on resources for health and education.
- **Dependency ratios** are high. The high number of non-earning family members per earner limits female participation in the labour force and may keep older children out of education, either to look after younger children and/or to work to supplement family income.
- There is rapid growth in the numbers of *working age*, leading to pressures on governments to increase employment opportunities.
- There is increased **urbanization**, reflecting both the growth of population in urban areas and the **migration** of people from rural to urban areas, which between 1950 and 1990 is estimated to have accounted for 50 per cent of urban population growth.

A number of LDCs – for example, Brazil and Malaysia – have achieved high *per capita* rates of growth of income in the face of high rates of growth of population. *It cannot therefore be argued in a simplistic manner that rapid population growth prevents or impedes economic growth and development.* The causes of poverty are to be found in the inequalities, both national and international, identified in other chapters in this book.

Nevertheless, rapid population growth does make development more difficult for the reasons given above. The problem of poverty is not merely one of numbers of people; it also involves issues relating to **quality of life** and material well-being. *Population and developmental issues are inseparable from one another.*

Development and the environment

> 'The protection of the environment is an essential part of development. Without adequate environmental protection, development is undermined; without development, resources will be inadequate for needed investments, and environmental protection will fail.'
> World Bank, 1992

Some environmental problems are linked to the lack of economic development. In many poor countries, problems associated with lack of clean water and inadequate sanitation, indoor air pollution from the burning of wood, straw and animal dung (so-called 'biomass fuels'), and many types of land degradation such as erosion, waterlogging and salinization, are the direct result of poverty.

Other problems are the result of, or are exacerbated by, the growth of economic activity. Such problems include industrial and energy-related pollution, deforestation caused by commercial logging, and the overuse of water –all resulting from economic expansion that fails to take account of the value of the environment. In these cases, environmental effects have to be built into the decision-making process.

Rapid population growth makes it more difficult to deal with many environmental problems, and poverty and environmental degradation mutually reinforce one another.

For example, poor farmers without access to sufficient land may cultivate erosion-prone hillsides and move into tropical forest areas where crop yields on cleared fields usually fall dramatically after a few years. The search for firewood leads to the loss of trees and ground cover.

Environmental economics

Many **environmental effects** are not directly reflected in prices and hence do not influence decisions based on the market.

Externalities are an important category of environmental effect. For example, a factory may discharge a toxic chemical into a river, killing fish and making the river dangerous or insanitary. This adversely affects users of the river, who thus suffer from an **external diseconomy**.

A *beneficial externality* or *external economy* is when the actions of one party have a beneficial effect on others and for which they do not pay.

Environmental economics argues that *the environment can be seen as a form of capital which produces a flow of goods and services to humankind.* The environment:

- is a source of raw materials and energy, some of which are renewable but others of which are finite;
- absorbs the waste products of human life through its air, soil and water;
- serves a variety of other functions to humankind, including life support, health and amenity.

The notion that the environment is a form of capital means that, if the services derived from it are not to be depleted, environmental assets must be maintained intact or renewed when used up or degraded. Some environmental assets *can* be renewed or restored after use – for example, forests and farmland. Other environmental assets (oil or minerals) can be *substituted for* by manufactured capital which generates an income stream: revenues generated from oil can be invested in financial assets or used to develop both physical and human capital. Some environmental capital is, however, irreplaceable once lost or degraded – wilderness ecology, virgin tropical forest.

The idea that we can replace environmental assets by replicating or compensating projects is at the heart of the notion of **sustainable development** (see Chapter 2, page 11) and depends on putting values on environmental functions.

- In theory, all environmental externalities, whether positive or negative, can be given a price. This is the **'polluter pays'** principle. Once this is applied, prices and incentives can be fixed in order to encourage desirable behaviour towards the environment and to penalize its abuse.
- In practice, a market-based solution to environmental problems in LDCs would be extremely difficult to design and to enforce, and there is *so far little evidence that Third World countries are prepared to adopt market solutions to environmental problems.*

Conclusions

Population, the environment and development are intimately linked to one another. In 1992 the World Bank estimated that as total population grew between then and the year 2030, global food production would have to *double*, and industrial output and energy use *triple* worldwide and increase *fivefold* in developing countries. The Bank concluded:

> 'This growth brings with it the risk of appalling environmental damage. Alternatively, it could bring with it better environmental protection, cleaner air and water, and the virtual elimination of acute poverty. Policy choices will make the difference.'

```
┌─────────────────────────────────────────────────────────┐
│                      KEY WORDS                            │
│  Population growth        Urbanization                    │
│  Fertility                Migration                       │
│  Birth rates              Quality of life                 │
│  Death rates              Environmental effects           │
│  Infant mortality         Externalities                   │
│  Life expectancy          External diseconomy             │
│  Demographic transition   Sustainable development         │
│  Dependency ratio         'Polluter pays' principle       │
└─────────────────────────────────────────────────────────┘
```

Reading list

Burningham, D., and Davies, J., *Green Economics*, Heinemann Educational, 1995.

Essay topics

1. 'The depletion of the Brazilian rainforests is a simple illustration of the fact that the global pursuit of economic growth will soon impoverish us all.'

   'Economic growth is the only way to reduce poverty in the developing countries.'

   Discuss critically these two statements. [100 marks]

   [University of London Examinations and Assessment Council 1993]

2. 'Economic growth should be curbed worldwide to reduce the impact of negative externalities on the world economy.'

   'Economic growth is necessary to increase living standards in both developed and developing countries.'

   (a) Explain the meaning of each of these statements. [50 marks]

   (b) Analyse the extent to which economic growth may increase or decrease economic welfare. [50 marks]

   [University of London Examinations and Assessment Council 1993]

Chapter Seven
Agricultural and industrial development

'For the newly emerging countries of the post-war period, industrialization was seen as synonymous with development, and development implied catching up with the advanced countries, using basically the same means.' United Nations Industrial Development Organization

According to the World Bank:

> *'Agriculture is the basic industry for the world's poorest countries, employing approximately 70–80 per cent of the labour force of low-income developing countries and accounting for roughly 35–40 per cent of GDP.'*

The share of agriculture in national income generally declines as *per capita* incomes rise, for two reasons. First, people spend a decreasing percentage of incomes on food as incomes rise; and secondly, as farmers increase the productivity of their land and labour, the share of a country's resources required to grow food for the rest of the population decreases.

Because of this relative decline in the importance of agriculture as *per capita* incomes rise, industry has been perceived to be the **leading sector** in development. Many countries have adopted negative policies towards agriculture, with the emphasis on transferring investible resources from the rural/agricultural to the urban/industrial sector. *This view has now been revised and the transformation of the agricultural sector is seen as both a cause and a consequence of successful development.*

Links between agricultural and industrial development
The *agricultural sector* plays a strategic role in the development of the industrial sector:

- The agricultural sector provides a major market for manufactured goods, both inputs required for the transformation of agriculture (pumps for agricultural irrigation systems, implements, chemical fertilizers) and consumer goods (bicycles, radios, household utensils, cigarettes) which farmers increasingly demand as their incomes rise.

- Agriculture satisfies the food requirements of the increasing urban population.
- Agriculture releases labour and capital for the industrial sector. Labour migrates to the urban/industrial sector and savings are extracted in various ways – through taxation and voluntary saving, for example, or through forced extraction (as was the case in the former Soviet Union).
- Agricultural exports earn the foreign exchange required for the importation of machinery and equipment and intermediate inputs (for example, oil, chemicals) required for development.
- Agriculture provides many of the industrial sector's inputs – cotton, sisal, tobacco.

The *industrial sector* in turn supports agriculture:

- Industry provides the inputs required for agricultural modernization (tractors, fertilizers).
- Industry provides a market for a part of agricultural output through the processing and manufacture of foodstuffs for both domestic consumption and exports.

The contributions that agriculture can make to development illustrate some difficult choices that governments have to make when defining development policies and objectives. First, high prices may persuade farmers to produce and sell more, but low food prices benefit urban consumers and minimize inflationary pressures. Secondly, promotion of export crops increases foreign exchange earnings, but this might be at the expense of producing foodstuffs for the domestic market. Thirdly, taxation of the agricultural sector may be necessary to raise revenue to finance government expenditure, but higher taxes may act as a disincentive to farmers who may produce less and/or consume more of what they produce.

Structural change

As noted above, as *per capita* incomes grow, there is a consistent decline in the share of the agricultural sector in national output, and a consistent increase in the share of the industrial sector.

The third major sector – *services* – has a less consistent pattern, although in higher income economies the service sector grows at the expense of the industrial sector. Table 9 presents data on sectoral shares of GDP for 1970 and 1985, with projections to the year 2000.

The sectoral distribution of the labour force changes less dramatically, although employment data are less comprehensive and reliable.

Table 9 Sectoral origin of world market economy production: historical and projected, 1970–2000 (percentage shares of GDP)*

Country group	Agriculture			Industry						Services		
				Total			Manufactures					
	1970	1985	2000	1970	1985	2000	1970	1985	2000	1970	1985	2000
Developed market	4.4	3.6	3.1	40.6	36.9	34.8	25.7	25.3	24.0	55.0	59.5	62.1
Developing countries	20.7	16.9	13.8	41.3	36.1	39.8	15.1	18.8	23.0	38.0	47.0	46.4
Petroleum exporters	15.0	13.6	12.5	61.0	44.6	45.0	5.6	9.4	9.8	24.0	41.8	42.5
Major manufacturers exporters	26.6	17.3	11.5	31.0	36.0	43.0	21.8	25.8	32.0	42.4	46.8	45.4
Other manufacturers oriented	16.6	15.2	13.8	32.6	32.3	34.8	21.8	21.5	23.4	50.8	52.5	54.1
Primary commodities exporters	26.3	23.8	19.1	30.7	24.9	34.2	11.4	10.9	20.6	43.0	36.1	46.7
Least developed countries	57.3	48.4	41.3	14.4	15.5	18.3	8.7	8.3	9.6	28.3	36.1	40.4

*Measured at 1980 prices and exchange rates. The agricultural sector comprises agriculture, forestry, hunting and fishing. The industrial sector comprises mining, manufacturing, construction, electricity, gas and water. All other branches of economic activity are categorized as services.

Source: United Nations, 1990

Table 10 Share of MVA of all developing countries (excluding China)

1975		1980		1985	
1 Brazil	17.3	Brazil	18.3	Brazil	16.00
2 Argentina	14.1	Mexico	11.6	Mexico	10.7
3 Mexico	11.0	Argentina	10.4	India	7.5
4 India	7.0	India	6.5	Argentina	7.4
5 Turkey	4.3	Korea, Rep. of	5.0	Korea, Rep. of	6.4
6 Korea, Rep. of	3.5	Taiwan	4.6	Taiwan	5.4
7 Taiwan	3.2	Turkey	3.4	Turkey	4.3
8 Iran	2.8	Venezuela	2.6	Iran	2.9
9 Venezuela	2.7	Philippines	2.3	Indonesia	2.9
10 Philippines	2.3	Iran	2.3	Cuba	2.7
11 Colombia	2.3	Indonesia	2.3	Saudi Arabia	2.5
12 Cuba	2.0	Colombia	2.1	Venezuela	2.4
13 Peru	1.9	Saudi Arabia	2.1	Thailand	2.0
14 Saudi Arabia	1.8	Thailand	1.8	Colombia	1.9
15 Puerto Rico	1.5	Hong Kong	1.6	Philippines	1.9
Subtotals	77.7		76.9		76.9

Source: Industrial Statistics Database, United Nations Industrial Development Organization (Vienna)

For all groups of LDCs, the industrial sector's share of the total labour force is less than its share of national output. This is a reflection both of the concentration of under-employed, low-productivity labour in the agricultural sector, and of the general use of capital-intensive methods of production in the 'modern' industrial sector.

Strategies of industrialization
The LDCs have gradually increased their share of global 'manufacturing value-added' (MVA) over the past two decades. In 1970 the LDCs accounted for about 11 per cent of global MVA; by 1993 their share had increased to an estimated 17 per cent (these figures exclude China for which separate estimates are made).

The experience of industrialization in the Third World is highly uneven. Although the large Latin American economies remain the most industrialized in absolute terms, the most rapidly industrializing economies are located in East and South East Asia. Table 10 illustrates how the distribution of Third World MVA has shifted in favour of the latter region.

Import-substituting industrialization (ISI)
ISI is a strategy of industrialization based on the domestic production of goods that were previously imported. It was initiated in many Latin

American economies as a response to two world wars, and the intervening global depression when either imports were not available or there was insufficient foreign exchange to pay for them.

After the ending of the Second World War in 1945, and with the achievement of political independence, many countries adopted ISI strategies (for example, India, Pakistan, Indonesia, and in the 1960s countries such as Nigeria, Kenya and Ghana). Typically the strategy involved the imposition of **tariffs** and other controls on imports to provide a protected domestic market for new domestic firms, (**infant industries**), or the affiliates of transnational corporations (TNCs).

The process began with the domestic production of *consumer goods* such as shoes, and the importation of *investment goods* such as shoe-making machines and *intermediate goods* (leather, plastics, etc.). In theory, once consumer goods have been substituted, the next 'round' of ISI would concentrate on machinery and equipment (investment goods) and finally on to *capital goods* (machines that can make other machines).

These expectations were not realized in practice. In the early 1960s, for example, Brazil appeared to have 'exhausted' the consumer goods stage of ISI without moving smoothly into the next stage. Economic growth slowed, inflation accelerated and social unrest grew. The Brazilian military staged a coup in 1964. This experience was not unique to Brazil but was repeated in many other countries – Argentina, Pakistan, Indonesia, Nigeria to name a few. *It was concluded that ISI had failed as an industrialization strategy.*

The *orthodox* explanation for the apparent failure was that there had been too much government intervention in the market mechanism (see 'Alternative theoretical perspectives on development' in Chapter 3). In particular, high tariff levels and overvalued exchange rates had discriminated against these countries' exports (for many the major export sector was agriculture) and had led to the creation of a high-cost, inefficient, uncompetitive domestic manufacturing sector.

Structuralist explanations focused on a variety of factors:

- continued shortages of foreign exchange – the balance-of-payments constraint on development;
- the dependence on foreign technology – considered 'inappropriate' to the resources and needs of LDCs;
- the inability of ISI to break or relax the various structural constraints or bottlenecks characteristic of the LDC economy.

Export-oriented industrialization (EOI)

At the same time that ISI appeared to be breaking down, a number of East and South East Asian economies – Singapore, Hong Kong, South Korea and Taiwan – were emerging as increasingly important exporters of manufactured goods.

The development strategies of these economies were based upon:

- outward-oriented trade policies that provided incentives which favoured neither the domestic market nor the export market (neutrality);
- the use of labour-intensive technologies in the manufacturing sector, consistent with factor endowments and comparative advantage;
- reliance on the market for a more efficient allocation of resources;
- minimal government intervention (see the box 'The East Asian Miracle').

THE EAST ASIAN 'MIRACLE'

The World Bank has argued that the key to the success of the East Asian economies is to be found in their sound and stable macroeconomic management ('getting prices right') and their rapid and sustained accumulation of physical and human capital.

The Bank accepts that there was government intervention in these economies, but argues that the prerequisites for successful government intervention are so rigorous that other economies cannot and should not attempt to follow the East Asian 'model'. The prerequisites include the following:

- There should be clear performance criteria for selective intervention, with monitoring of performance.
- The costs of intervention, both direct and indirect, must not become excessive. In particular, price distortions arising from intervention must not become too extreme.

The World Bank maintains that government intervention was in effect 'market-friendly', creating an environment that promoted investment in people, competition among firms and an economy open to international trade.

Source: Adapted from *The East Asian Miracle: Economic Growth and Public Policy*, Oxford University Press for the World Bank, 1993

That these economies have been very successful is not open to doubt. The original four economies have been joined by a number of other Newly Industrializing Economies (NIEs) – Malaysia, Thailand, Indonesia and China – in what has become the most dynamic and rapidly growing region in the world, the Asia Pacific Region.

However, economists argue over how these economies have succeeded. The orthodox explanation emphasizes the importance of the free market and international trade. The critics of this view emphasize the important role that the state has played in the economic life in all these countries, most notably in Taiwan and South Korea.

SOUTH KOREA

The American economist Alice Amsden, in her book *Asia's Next Giant: South Korea and Late Industrialisation* (Oxford University Press, 1989), emphasizes the strategic role of the Korean state in what she calls **late industrialization**. She argues, somewhat provocatively, that the state has *deliberately* got prices 'wrong' – for example, subsidized credit provided to sectors considered important by the government – in order to achieve its development objectives.

Apart from the interventionist state, the major agent of expansion in late industrialization is the *modern industrial enterprise*. In Korea, this is the *chaebol*, a large diversified business group which has penetrated the lower end of numerous foreign markets and has supplanted the need for foreign firms to undertake investments in targeted industries. (Amsden argues that Korea has depended heavily on foreign loans but that there has been relatively little direct foreign investment, except in a number of relatively labour-intensive sectors.)

The *chaebol* themselves have increasingly invested overseas, with Samsung, Daewoo, Hyundai and LG (formerly Lucky Goldstar) leading the way (*Financial Times*, 10 February 1995).

Amsden and other writers on South Korea emphasize the role of the developmental state, the growth of indigenous capital and the possibilities for capitalist development in so-called 'peripheral countries'. The shift by South Korea in the 1970s into heavy industries (engineering, shipbuilding, industrial chemicals, automobiles) and the increasing innovative capabilities of the *chaebol* (based on increasing research and development expenditures and a commitment to education, especially technical and scientific) provide support to those who argue that the notion of dependency is static and ahistorical, and that independent industrialization is possible in the Third World.

Conclusions

The record of industrialization in the Third World is mixed. When successful, industrialization transforms the structure of the economy and leads to sustained economic growth. To be successful, however, industrialization requires a stable macroeconomic environment and the simultaneous promotion of agricultural development.

The lessons from the East Asian experience seem to be the following:

- Direct but selective government intervention is needed, both to create new productive capacity and to ensure that existing capacity is used efficiently.
- There has to be investment in human capital formation, with special emphasis on scientific and technical education and training.
- There has to be investment in research and development (R&D) activities.
- Appropriate institutions have to be created to overcome specific market failures that inhibit industrial development – quality assurance, training, information collection, technology diffusion, testing and research support institutes.

KEY WORDS

Leading sector	Infant industries
Structural change	Export-oriented
Import-substituting	industrialization
industrialization	Late industrialization
Tariffs	

Essay topics

1. 'The Zimbabwe United Passenger Company (ZUPCO) has placed its largest ever order for the parts of 296 conventional buses from the Netherlands and 80 minibuses from Japan. The buses will be assembled in Zimbabwe' (*Financial Gazette*, 28 March 1991).

(a) Why might it be advantageous to a developing country such as Zimbabwe to assemble vehicles rather than purchase completed vehicles? [10 marks]

(b) Both types of buses are operated by one person, but the conventional buses hold more passengers. Use economic analysis to explain why the bus company might find it appropriate to order both types of vehicle. [15 marks]

[University of Cambridge Local Examinations Syndicate 1993]

2. Explain how famine could be the outcome of the operation of the law of diminishing returns. In recent years, the growth of world grain production has generally matched, and in advanced countries exceeded, population growth. In the light of this, discuss what might be done to avoid or reduce the impact of famines in the future. [25 marks]
[Joint Matriculation Board 1992]

Data Response Question

This task is based on a question set in a specimen paper by the University of London Examinations and Assessment Council. Read the article entitled 'Economic miracle or myth?' which appeared in *The Economist* on 2 October 1993. Then answer the questions.

Economic miracle or myth?

Economists have long debated the proper role of government intervention in developing economies. The remarkable economic success of Japan and other East Asian countries, which are known to have pursued interventionist policies, has been seized upon by some economists as evidence that the so-called 'East Asian model' is a better way to foster growth than orthodox free-market medicine. To resolve the question of whether government intervention did help to boost growth in East Asia, the World Bank has just published a vast 390-page study, 'The East Asian miracle'.

The Bank has scrutinised the performance of eight East Asian 'superstars'. Hong Kong, Indonesia, Japan, Malaysia, Singapore, South Korea, Taiwan and Thailand. Since 1965 those economies have together grown at an annual rate of 5.5 percent, more than twice as fast as the rest of East Asia and three times as fast as Latin America. The export performance of these East Asian economies has been particularly dramatic, with their share of world exports of manufactures leaping from 9 percent in 1965 to 21 percent in 1990.

Not only did the eight economies grow rapidly, they were also successful in sharing the fruits of growth, with low and declining inequality of income.

What was the secret of this economic miracle? The Bank's exhaustive report which characteristically tries to tip-toe delicately between the rival camps, offers crumbs for everybody. Supporters of the East Asian model have been quick to leap on one of the Bank's conclusions: that most of these countries did not pursue pure free-market policies, but followed interventionist policies, sometimes with success. Free marketeers, by contrast, can take comfort from the warning the Bank gives that, if other developing countries try to take the interventionist route, they are unlikely to enjoy the same success as the East Asian countries.

There is not a simple recipe for East Asia's success, for, as the World Bank points out, there was no single Asian economic model. The eight countries pursued a diverse mix of policies with varying degrees of intervention.

Hong Kong has followed the most free-market policies of almost any country in the world; Japan and South Korea saw the most heavy-handed intervention; while the newest tigers, Indonesia and Thailand, have followed far less activist policies.

However, the eight countries did have one thing in common; they **got the economic fundamentals right,** with low inflation, sound fiscal policies, high levels of domestic savings, heavy investment in education; and they kept their economies more open to foreign technology than most other developing countries. In the past 30 years, for example, inflation averaged 8 percent in the East Asian superstars, well below the 18 percent average in other developing countries. This provided the best possible climate for long-term investment. To this extent, there was no economic 'miracle'; East Asia's success simply reflects sound economics.

East Asian economies thrived because governments used a mix of policies to achieve higher investment than elsewhere in human and physical capital. Public spending on education was not much higher in East Asia than elsewhere, but where these eight countries excelled was that a bigger share of that spending was allocated to basic primary and secondary education, vital for a skilled workforce, rather than to universities.

Likewise, during the past two decades private-sector investment as a share on GDP has been almost twice as high in East Asia as in other developing countries. This was partly thanks to a more stable macroeconomic climate – low inflation and less volatile interest rates – but, says the World Bank, some intervention, in the shape of tax incentives, subsidies and cheap loans, must take some of the credit.

The most ambitious interventions in East Asia were industrial policies to promote specific sectors. The World Bank concludes that these mostly failed.

However, the World Bank reckons that two other types of intervention were successful: export promotion and directed credit. Most countries pursued

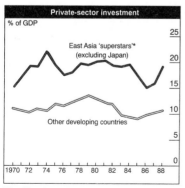

*Hong Kong, Indonesia, Japan, Malaysia, Singapore, South Korea, Taiwan, Thailand

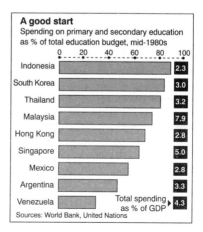

aggressive export promotion policies (subsidies, favoured access to foreign borrowing and foreign exchange). The focus on foreign markets imposed strong discipline on firms and encouraged efficiency.

The World Bank also finds evidence that governments' manipulation of interest rates may have enhanced growth. Governments in Japan, South Korea, Malaysia, Taiwan and Thailand intervened to reduce the cost of capital for firms and directed credit to favoured industries.

The World Bank gives warning that successful intervention does depend on an institutional factor: the competence and relative lack of corruptibility of civil servants.

1. The author of the passage states that the eight countries in East Asia 'got the economic fundamentals right'. Examine the significance of these factors in explaining the rapid rate of their economic growth. [25 marks]

2. Explain why (i) some types of intervention might be unsuccessful in promoting economic growth, and (ii) other types might be successful in promoting economic growth. [10 marks]

3. Examine the problems which might be associated with such a rapid rate of economic growth. [15 marks]

Chapter Eight

International trade and economic development

'TRADE, NOT AID' – a popular development slogan

Does trade lead to development?

The poor countries are **open economies** with imports and exports accounting for a large proportion of national output.

Output and employment levels and rates of growth are highly dependent on export performance. Imports of machinery and equipment, fuels and raw materials are essential inputs for the development process.

During the colonial period the colonies were a captive market for the manufactured goods of the metropolitan powers, while in return supplying raw materials and tropical foodstuffs. For the poorest countries, in particular, *these patterns of trade have changed only slowly.* Given the specific problems of those countries dependent on **primary commodity exports,** it is not surprising that the system of international trade is sometimes seen to be inherently unfair to the poorer countries.

Orthodox trade theory – the theory of **comparative advantage** – predicts that all countries can benefit by specializing in the production and trade of those commodities in which they have the lowest relative production costs; differences in comparative costs are based on inter-country differences in factor endowments. Poor countries with an abundance of labour and a scarcity of capital should specialize in the production and export of *labour-intensive* commodities, while rich countries with plentiful capital and scarce labour should specialize in *capital-intensive* commodities.

LDC trade

The stereotypical picture of trade is of LDCs exporting primary products (agricultural and mineral products) to the industrial economies in return for manufactured goods. *In practice, developed economies export significant quantities of primary products (especially temperate foodstuffs) and the LDCs export manufactured goods.*

Table 11 illustrates the changes that have occurred in the structure of LDC exports over the 1955–89 period.

Table 11 The share structure of LDC exports: selected years

	1955	1960	1970	1980	1989
Total exports	100	100	100	100	100
Food	36.5	33.6	26.5	10.6	11.1
Agricultural raw materials	20.5	18.3	10.0	7.3	7.6
Fuels, minerals, ores	35.1	38.5	45.2	50.7	23.2
Manufactures	7.7	9.2	17.7	21.5	56.9
Total non-fuel, mineral exports	100	100	100	100	100
Food	56.4	55.0	48.9	26.9	14.7
Agricultural raw materials	31.7	30.0	18.5	18.5	10.0
Manufactures	11.9	15.0	32.6	54.6	75.3

Table 12 Percentage of developing country exports and imports by country group

	1958	1965	1970	1980	1989
Exports to:					
Developed market economies	72.2	71.1	73.8	68.4	62.1
Developing countries	23.1	21.0	19.6	26.4	32.7
Centrally planned economies	3.4	6.6	5.6	3.9	4.1
Other	1.3	0.7	0.0	1.3	1.1
Imports from:					
Developed market economies	74.7	71.3	72.0	63.4	60.7
Developing countries	20.8	20.2	19.1	29.7	32.9
Centrally planned economies	4.5	8.5	8.9	6.9	6.4

Table 12 shows the changes that have occurred in the direction of LDC trade. The developed market economies still dominate but they account for a declining proportion of LDC exports and imports. Trade between the LDCs has expanded although, as of 1989, it still accounted for only one-third of the total.

Many LDCs are dependent on a small number of types of export. For example:

- tobacco and gold account for over 40 per cent of Zimbabwe's exports;
- coffee and petroleum account for 37 per cent of Colombia's exports;
- bauxite and alumina account for 52 per cent of Jamaica's exports.

However, two examples can be given of the changes that have occurred:

- *Bangladesh:* In 1972, jute products accounted for 90 per cent of total exports; by 1991, the share of jute had fallen to 18 per cent and ready-made garments accounted for over 50 per cent of the total.
- *Mauritius:* In 1976, sugar accounted for 72 per cent of total exports; by 1991, sugar's share had fallen to 29 per cent and clothing and textiles accounted for 55 per cent of the total.

LDCs continue to dominate world trade in certain commodities – petroleum, sugar, coffee, copper, rubber, tin, tea, palm oil, bananas – but this dominance/dependence can be seen as a weakness rather than as a strength. Primary commodity prices appear to be prone to a long-term decline relative to other prices, and instability – fluctuations around the trend – has increased in the 1980s (Figure 5).

There has been a remarkable change in the composition of developing countries' exports, with manufactures accounting for almost 57 per cent of total exports in 1989. But many developing countries, especially the 47 least developed countries, remain heavily dependent on primary commodity exports (especially tropical beverages, agricultural raw materials and minerals, ore and metals). Since 1980, the markets for these commodities have remained depressed, despite some short-term rises in prices in these unstable markets. In addition the

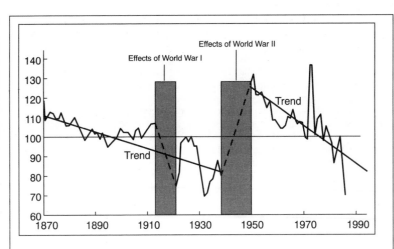

Figure 5 Real commodity prices deflated by price of manufactures 1870–1986 (1980 = 100)

Source: ODI/IMF, 1988

THE URUGUAY ROUND, MARKET ACCESS, AND THE DEVELOPING COUNTRIES

For each of the 118 participants in the **Uruguay Round**, the increase in national income resulting from the successful conclusions of the Round will come from two principal sources:

- more efficient use of domestic resources when domestic distortions, such as trade barriers, are reduced or removed;
- increased access to markets of trading partners.

It is estimated that implementation of the market-access provisions of the Round could add between $200 billion and $300 billion (in 1992 dollars) annually to world income. These figures are probably an underestimate; *they do not include services, and no attempt has yet been made to capture the effects on productivity growth of greater openness in trade.*

Even at the 'underestimated' level, full implementation of the Uruguay Round could boost the GDP of developing economies by almost $80 billion (in 1992 dollars) a year. Developing country gains from agricultural liberalization alone are estimated at between $20 billion and $60 billion a year, depending on the extent of each economy's liberalization.

Improved market access for agricultural and industrial products will result primarily from broad reductions in tariffs and more control of quantitative restrictions and subsidies. In contrast to the situation for industrial products, increased market access for agricultural products will involve limiting the use of domestic support policies. Reduction of export subsidies by industrial countries will boost the competitiveness of exports from developing countries.

The effect of the reduction in **most-favoured-nation** (MFN) tariffs on individual suppliers depends on whether the importing country gives the product MFN, preferential, or free-trade treatment. For MFN imports there is an unambiguous increase in the volume of sales in the importing country following a tariff reduction. In the case of imports already receiving preferential or free-trade-area treatment, the reduction in MFN tariff rates can reduce margins of preference, inducing buyers to switch to competing suppliers. Analysers suggest that the trade gains from reductions in MFN tariff rates are likely to outweigh the losses from preference erosion, even for exporters receiving preferences.

The reduction in duties that apply to developing countries is estimated at 34 per cent – less than the 38 per cent reduction on industrial products from all sources – and the figures for clothing and footwear (of particular interest to developing countries) are even lower. Nevertheless, the effects on **trade creation** will be large even for such products because existing tariff rates on them are the highest, and the percentage decline in the tariff-inclusive price in importing countries will be substantial. Moreover, where a quantitative restriction (rather than the tariff) is the binding restraint under the Multi-Fibre Arrangement, the extent of the increase in market access may be larger than the cut in the tariff alone would indicate.

A disappointing result of the agreement is that tariff escalation will continue for agricultural products. It was hoped that discrimination against processed commodities would be reduced, thus enhancing strategies for natural resource-based industrialization. But the agreed reductions in tariffs, whether viewed in absolute or percentage terms, do not clearly rise or fall with the level of processing.

Source: *World Bank Annual Report 1994*

majority of international commodity agreements have fallen into disarray. Attempts at diversification by the smaller, poorer, primary commodity exporting economies have typically not been successful, and even after the completion of the **Uruguay Round** (see the box), barriers to trade are still significant.

Terms of trade

Terms of trade refers to the value of one bundle of commodities in terms of another. In developing economies, attention has been focused on the behaviour of **net barter terms of trade**. A NBTT is a price index of exports divided by a price index of imports, expressed as a percentage:

$$\text{Net barter terms of trade} = (P_E/P_I) \times 100.$$

If the price of exports is falling relative to the price of imports (or if the price of exports is rising less rapidly than the price of imports) then the NBTT is deteriorating; that is, a given bundle of exports buys a smaller bundle of imports.

Many economists have argued that the NBTTs of primary commodity exporters show a long-run (secular) tendency to deteriorate. Various reasons were put forward as to why this should be the case:

- In the developed industrialized economies, powerful trades unions are able to capture the benefits of productivity gains, whereas in LDCs, higher productivity in the primary commodity sector leads to lower prices.
- Income elasticities of demand for agricultural producers decline as income rises, so that demand for them grows more slowly than demand for manufactured goods.
- Technological advances have led to the development of synthetic substitutes for many primary commodities – for example, plastics substituted for rubber, synthetic fibres substituted for cotton and wool.
- Technological changes have reduced the weight of metal and other minerals required to produce a unit of manufactured goods. There has also been a change in the composition of manufactured output, away from heavy industries (iron and steel, shipbuilding) towards newer activities less dependent of raw materials (e.g. electronics).
- The protection of agricultural sectors in the developed economies has created exportable surpluses of some agricultural commodities and reduced import demands for others. For example, sugar beet has been produced at the expense of sugar cane imports.

Table 13 Net barter terms of trade (1980 = 100)

			LCDs			
				Other LDCs		
	DCs	All	Major petroleum exporters	All	Major exporters of manufactures	Remaining countries
1980	100	100	100	100	100	100
1985	101	96	101	91	97	87
1990	111	75	65	82	88	79

Source: United Nations Conference on Trade and Development (UNCTAD): reproduced in David Colman and Frederick Nixson, *Economics of Change in Less Developed Countries*, 3rd edn, Harvester Wheatsheaf, 1994

These are all convincing arguments supporting the hypothesis, but the empirical evidence does not provide unambiguous support. Much depends on the time period covered and the country and commodity coverage.

There have been short periods, in 1973–76 and 1979–81, when the NBTTs moved in favour of primary producers, but there were longer periods in which changes in NBTTs favoured the developed economies. For all LDCs, there was an improvement in NBTT over the period 1960–90 of around 65 per cent, despite a dramatic reduction by a third from the 1981 peak. But this improvement was largely owing to changes in export prices for oil. When the major petroleum exporters are excluded from the series (column 4 of Table 13), NBTT shows a decline of some 20 per cent over the 1960–90 period.

Short-run earnings instability

It is argued that the prices of primary commodities are more unstable in the short run than those of manufactured goods. This in turn gives rise to short-run instability of export earnings, which are damaging to the growth and development prospects of primary commodity exporters.

Most, though not all, poor countries are **price-takers** on the world markets for their exports. That is, the production of primary commodity exports in individual countries is generally small in relation to international production. The price instability of primary commodities is attributable to:

- the competitive nature of world commodity markets;
- the relatively inelastic price elasticities of supply and demand, with shifts in the supply or demand curves requiring large price changes to restore market equilibrium;

- the vulnerability of agriculture to adverse weather conditions;
- fluctuations in demand in the industrial countries for primary commodities;
- the agricultural policies of the industrial countries restricting market access and – through the use of quotas and controlled prices – reducing the size of the 'free' market.

International commodity agreements

Large fluctuations in the export earnings of developing countries may be caused by:

- excessive variability of supply and demand;
- low price elasticity of supply and demand;
- excessive specialization on one or two commodities;
- the concentration of exports in particular markets.

The empirical evidence on export-earning instability is inconclusive and does not suggest that developing countries as a group suffer extreme instability as a result of their dependence on primary products. Some commodities, however, such as cocoa, copper and cotton, have experienced significant earnings instability, and from this it follows that individual developing countries may well have had their development prospects affected by such instability.

Earnings instability may arise from either the demand side or the supply side.

Demand fluctuations are beyond the control of the exporting countries and reflect changes in the level of economic activity in the industrialized countries. Further, a proportionate reduction in demand will tend to have a greater adverse affect upon the total export earnings from a commodity than an equivalent proportionate supply increase.

Demand fluctuations have been large – the world economic boom of 1972–74 and the subsequent recession of 1975–83, for example. Developing countries have argued that they should be compensated for the damage caused to their economies.

If variations in *supply* are the major cause of export earnings instability, stabilizing prices will not stabilize earnings. Stable prices would reduce earnings in times of scarcity and increase then in times of glut. Much will depend on the *price elasticities* of demand and supply.

There are various types of **international commodity agreements**.

- Buffer stock schemes

These operate by buying the commodity when the price falls below some agreed minimum level and selling the commodity when price rises above the agreed maximum level (Figure 6).

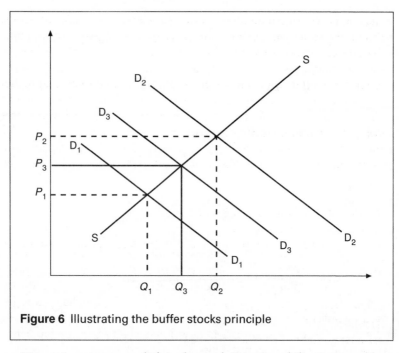

Figure 6 Illustrating the buffer stocks principle

Figure 6 represents a shift in demand. Price instability is caused by a shift in the demand line from D_1D_1 to D_2D_2. At D_3D_3, buffer stocks come into action. P_3 is the equilibrium price at which quantity demanded equals quantity supplied (both equal Q_3). If the actual price rises above P_3, say to P_2, then the buffer stock authorities will sell $Q_2 - Q_3$ in order to reduce price to P_3. If price falls to P_1, then the authorities buy $Q_3 - Q_1$ in order to raise price to P_3. In this case, price stabilization implies revenue stabilization.

When the supply curve shifts the analysis becomes more complicated, because we then have to take into account the elasticity of demand. As a general rule, the more inelastic is the demand curve, the greater is the variation in price stabilization.

Upper and lower price levels must be realistic, and the buffer stock authorities must have adequate resources to defend the lower price level when necessary. Often this is not the case and funds are exhausted attempting to defend unrealistic minimum prices. Both the International Cocoa Agreement in 1981 and the International Tin Agreement in 1985 collapsed for this reason.

● Quota agreements
These schemes attempt to restrict supply in order to maintain the pur-

chasing power of commodity exports in relation to industrial goods. Producer nations get together to form a **cartel** and agree to restrict production and exports by the allocation of a quota to each member of the agreement.

There are often arguments over the allocation of quotas, and higher prices will tend to increase supply and create pressures for members to cheat. Consumers will also have an incentive to buy at lower prices either from non-member countries or illicitly from members. The International Coffee Agreement (now defunct) and the Organization of Petroleum Exporting Countries (OPEC) are examples of such arrangements.

● International compensatory finance

Rather than attempt to stabilize individual commodity prices, these schemes try to increase the level and stability of earnings from total exports.

The Lome Convention, which is an agreement between the European Union (EU) and a number of African, Caribbean and Pacific (ACP) countries, has an export-earning stabilization scheme called STABEX. This applies to unexpected falls in export earnings of a selected number of products from ACP to the EU.

The International Monetary Fund (IMF) operates a more general compensatory financing facility which, since 1988, has been called the Compensatory and Contingency Financial Facility (CCFF). This covers fluctuations in foreign exchange earnings resulting from a variety of factors – changes in export and import prices, interest rate changes, tourist receipts and migrants' remittances, etc. – to encourage member countries to undertake long-term programmes.

Manufactured goods exports

Changes in the structure of output are reflected in changes in a country's exports, so as countries industrialize we would expect to see changes in the composition of exports, with a rise in the proportion of exported manufactures.

This change can be seen in Table 11, but average figures for LDCs as a whole conceal the rise of the NIEs as major exporters of manufactured goods. The South and East Asian economies account for over 75 per cent of total LDC manufactured exports, with Taiwan and South Korea alone accounting for about 38 per cent. The LDCs have increased their share of global manufactured exports (from 5 per cent in 1970 to over 15 per cent in the late-1980s), but trade is still dominated by the developed economies which account for over 77 per cent of global manufactured exports. With respect to the direction of trade, the developed market economies largely trade with one another. Manufactured goods exports from the NIEs go largely to the developed economies, with less than 20 per cent of their manufactured exports going to other LDCs.

There have been changes in the composition of manufactured goods exports. The share of processed products has risen, and some of the NIEs are becoming important exporters of more sophisticated commodities embodying increasingly advanced technologies. Countries such as Singapore, Malaysia, Brazil, Indonesia, Morocco, the Philippines, Thailand, Tunisia and Turkey variously export chemical, medicinal and pharmaceutical products, electrical machinery and aircraft.

The more advanced NIEs, Taiwan and Korea in particular, faced with growing competition from lower-wage economies such as Indonesia and China, are moving to higher-valued production. This is in traditional areas, such as clothing, and in new priority sectors – computer peripherals, integrated circuits, mini- and macrocomputers, and automobiles. The Koreans in particular are having great success in these areas, and have acquired the necessary technologies both through direct foreign investment (DFI – see Chapter 9) and by their own efforts in increased research and development expenditures.

Conclusions

International trade is inherently neither good nor bad. It creates new opportunities, incomes and jobs but it can also destroy them as technologies change and new centres of production emerge.

International trade has a higher profile today than perhaps at any other time in the recent past. The Uruguay Round (see earlier) has important implications for LDC trade, and **trade liberalization** is an important component of the majority of programmes for LDC economic reform and adjustment. On the other hand, international cooperation through commodity agreements aimed at stabilizing primary commodity prices is minimal, and many poor countries are faced with both unstable and declining prices for their major exports.

Those countries that have begun the process of industrialization and the export of manufactured goods have fared best in terms of economic growth. Smaller poorer countries still heavily dependent on the export of a limited range of primary commodities have few options and will remain dependent on the global community for their sustenance.

KEY WORDS

Open economies	Instability
Primary commodity exports	Price-takers
Comparative advantage	International commodity
Uruguay Round	agreements
Most-favoured nation	Cartel
Trade creation	Trade liberalization
Net barter terms of trade	

Reading list
Maunder, P., *et al.*, Chapter 31 in *Economics Explained*, 3rd edn, Collins Educational, 1995.

Essay topics
1. 'In reality, the GATT Uruguay deal has created a new world trade order geared to the interests of industrialized countries and powerful transnational companies, consigning the world's poorest countries to a future of deepening poverty' (Oxfam). Discuss.
   [Oxford & Cambridge Schools Examination Board 1995]
2. Explain why the prices of primary products such as agricultural produce, raw materials and energy are often unstable. [25 marks]
   [Associated Examining Board 1992]
3. (a) Outline the theory of comparative advantage as applied to international trade. [13 marks]
   (b) In the light of this theory, comment on the view that the purchase of cheap imports from developing countries by developed countries should be reduced as it causes the exploitation of the workers in the developing countries and the unemployment of workers in the developed countries. [12 marks]
   [University of Cambridge Local Examinations Syndicate 1993]
4. Developing countries frequently depend heavily upon primary production.
   (a) What is meant by primary production and what are the problems caused by this dependency? [10 marks]
   (b) Discuss the difficulties faced by developing countries when they try to diversify their economies. [10 marks]
   [University of Cambridge Local Examinations Syndicate 1996]

Data Response Question

This task is based on a question set in a specimen paper by the University of London Examinations and Assessment Council. Read the article, which is adapted from *Economics* by D. Begg, S. Fischer and R. Dornbusch (McGraw-Hill, 1987). Then answer the questions.

Traditionally the less developed countries (LDCs) have sought to secure the gains from trade by exporting primary products to the rest of the world and using the revenue to obtain badly needed machinery and other manufactured imports. As late as 1960, exports of primary commodities accounted for 84 per cent of all LDC exports. Nevertheless, many LDCs have become sceptical of the route to development through specialization in the production of primary products. Today, less than half of all LDC exports are primary products.

The table below shows that, with the spectacular exception of petroleum, the trend in real prices of primary products has been downwards for the last two decades. This can be attributed to both increased supply and reduced demand.

The real price of primary products
(Index: 1950–59 = 100)

	1964–73	1974–83
33 commodities	82.8	78.4
Agricultural	78.3	79.0
Metals, minerals	101.6	73.1
Petroleum	60.5	344.6

A further disadvantage in concentrating on the production of primary products is that their real prices tend to be very volatile. A change of more than 40 per cent in the real price within a single year is not uncommon. In any particular year, LDCs are uncertain how many imports their export revenue is going to finance.

1. (a) Explain why the real prices of primary products 'tend to be very volatile' [6 marks]
   (b) Explain what is meant by 'the trend in real prices of primary products has been downwards for the last two decades'. [4 marks]
   (c) Carefully analyse the factors that might have accounted for the downward trend in the real prices of primary products. [8 marks]
2. Why might specialization in primary production in less developed countries be considered an unsatisfactory method of encouraging economic development? [7 marks]

Chapter Nine
Transnational corporations and economic development

'Multinationals have changed their ideas about where their competitive advantage lies. They used to think that their most precious resource was capital, and that the prime task of management was to allocate it in the most productive way. Now they have become convinced that their most precious resource is knowledge, and that the prime task of management is to ensure that their knowledge is generated as widely and used as efficiently as possible.'
The Economist, 24–30 June 1995

A transnational (or 'multinational') corporation (TNC) is an enterprise that owns *income-generating assets* such as mines, plantations, factories and sales offices in *different nation states*; that is, it engages in international production.

Unlike the national firm that exports all or part of its product, much of the trade of the TNC takes place within the corporation (**intra-corporate trade**) rather than between independent economic agents. Also, unlike the national firm that exports part of its factor inputs (material or human capital), the TNC, through **direct foreign investment** (DFI), supplies such inputs as a 'package' and maintains control of the use that is made of them.

It is estimated by the United Nations that by the beginning of the 1990s there were approximately 35 000 TNCs – that is **parent companies** – with between them approximately 150 000 **foreign affiliates** worldwide. Of that latter total, perhaps just over 40 per cent are located in developing countries.

Table 14 illustrates the growing importance of TNCs originating in the semi-industrialized countries, such as Brazil, Korea, China and Taiwan.

The majority of TNCs are relatively small or medium-sized companies. The TNC population is, however, dominated by a smaller group – perhaps 600 in total – of giant companies, each of which had global sales of more than $1 billion in the mid-1980s, and which together accounted for over 20 per cent of market-economy (developed and less developed) industrial and agricultural valued-added.

Table 14 The geographical distribution of parent transnational corporations and foreign affiliates: late 1970s–early 1990s

Region/economy	Parent corporations	Foreign affiliates*
Developed countries of which:	30 900	73 400
France	2 000	3 671
Germany	6 984	10 978
Japan	3 331	2 884
Switzerland	3 000	–
United Kingdom	1 533	3 411
USA	3 721	13 582
Developing countries of which:	3 800	62 900
Brazil	576	7 110
China	553	15 966
Hong Kong	500	2 464
India	176	926
Malaysia	153	578
Korea, Republic of	668	2 821
Taiwan	405	4 764
Central and Eastern Europe	300	10 900
World totals	35 000	147 200

*Represents the number of foreign affiliates as reported by host countries.
Source: United Nations, 1992

These very large TNCs dominate a number of key sectors – petroleum, chemicals, machinery and equipment, and motor vehicles. They include the best-known companies – General Motors, Ford, IBM, Toyota, General Electric, Unilever – as well as the petroleum giants.

Direct foreign investment

TNCs enter new markets largely through direct foreign investment, often using **joint-venture** arrangements in which they are either majority or minority **equity** holders. **Non-equity operations** include **licensing** and **franchising**, where the TNC is not an equity holder but where it can exercise control through, for example, the supply of technology or management.

The global stock of DFI in the early 1990s was estimated at $1.7 trillion. Of this total, 70 per cent was located in the EU, Japan and the USA. The USA is both the largest source of DFI and the largest recipient of inward DFI.

Table 15 Average annual inflows of foreign direct investment to the ten largest developing-economy recipients of foreign direct investment ($ billion)

Host economy	1970–79	Host economy	1980–90
Brazil	1.3	Singapore	2.3
Mexico	0.6	Mexico	1.9
Malaysia	0.3	Brazil	1.8
Nigeria	0.3	China	1.7
Singapore	0.3	Hong Kong	1.1
Egypt	0.3	Malaysia	1.1
Indonesia	0.2	Egypt	0.9
Hong Kong	0.1	Argentina	0.7
Iran	0.1	Thailand	0.7
Uruguay	0.1	Taiwan	0.5
Share of flows to developing countries (%)	66	Share of flows to developing countries (%)	68

Source: United Nations, 1992

In 1990, the LDCs received *inward flows* of DFI of US$31.9 billion. The Asian region was the largest recipient, with about 58 per cent of LDC inflows, followed by Latin America and the Caribbean with 32 per cent.

Among LDCs, the 'top ten' recipients of DFI account for almost 70 per cent of total LDC inflows. Table 15 lists the largest recipients for the periods 1970–79 and 1980–90. The rapidly growing, export-oriented industrializers – Singapore, Hong Kong, Malaysia, Thailand, Taiwan and China – dominate the picture along with the three large Latin American economies. Korea is not included in this list as it has generally attempted to restrict DFI, limiting it to joint ventures, and has depended heavily on licensing for technology acquisition.

Within the South East Asian region, a great deal of DFI flows between countries. For example, 40 per cent of DFI in Malaysia and 30 per cent in Thailand comes from other Asian economies, especially Korea and Taiwan. Enterprises from China are also beginning to invest in other countries on a large scale.

Why do LDCs want DFI?

Despite the reservations that many LDCs have had in the past concerning the role of foreign capital in the development process, competition between LDCs for TNC investment is probably greater now than ever before. This competition has been intensified by the

---

WHY DO TNCs INVEST IN LDCs?

In order to invest overseas, an enterprise must possess an advantage or asset not shared by its local competitors. In addition, it is the use of those assets or advantages within the enterprise – their **internalization** – that gives the TNC its unique advantages.

The competitive strengths of TNCs are obvious from what has already been said. Clearly TNCs have a preference for investing in already developed economies and the middle- or upper-income poorer economies. So what motivates TNC investments in poor countries?

The following factors are of importance:

- the exploitation of raw materials either not found in other countries or more cheaply available in poor countries – iron ore, bauxite, copper;
- the exploitation of the agricultural potential of the poor country via large-scale agribusiness – ranching, soya beans, pineapples, sugar;
- the exploitation of large and/or rapidly growing domestic markets via ISI (see Chapter 7) – cigarettes, soft drinks, automobiles, cosmetics – where it is important that TNCs establish themselves to safeguard their markets from competitors;
- the use of low-wage, non-unionized, often predominantly female labour in export processing zones (EPZs) in assembly or processing activities – electronics, garments.

Different types of DFI are influenced by differing economic factors. All TNCs, however, require political stability in host economies, with freedom from arbitrary expropriation and with the guarantee of profit repatriation.

---

changes that have occurred in Eastern and Central Europe and the former Soviet Union and by the emergence of China as a capital importer.

TNCs own, control or have access to vast resources of capital, technology and all kinds of expertise – financial, managerial, marketing – and often provide access to export markets. These are the factors that are absent or in short supply in LDCs, and the main attraction of TNC investment is that these resources are all part of the DFI 'package'. The TNC appears to be the 'engine of growth' that can solve the problems of underdevelopment and poverty.

Many radical economists would argue that precisely the opposite is the case; that TNCs exploit LDCs through the extraction of raw materials for which they do not pay a fair price, through their use of cheap labour, and through the transfer of 'inappropriate' technology and products. There are also well-documented cases of TNCs interfering in political affairs and destabilizing governments. Critics call this **neo-colonialism.**

Opinion has changed over the past 15 years, however. There is now wider agreement that TNCs can make an important contribution to development, although governments must create the conditions to ensure that the full potential of DFI for development is realized.

TNCs and development

● Technology transfer and employment

It is generally agreed that TNCs are the major channel for the transfer of new technologies to less-developed countries. But are those technologies 'appropriate' with respect to the resource endowments and development objectives of LDCs?

Bass commits $40m to China joint venture

TONY WALKER AND RODERICK ORAM

Bass, the large UK brewer, has committed $40m to a new joint venture with the Ginsber Beer Group in China's north-eastern Jilin province. This is the first significant UK investment in the world's fastest-growing beer market.

Bass will take a 55 per cent stake in Bass Ginsber Beer Company and plans to double output over the next five years. Ginsber, part of Hong Zui Corporation, a township enterprise, will contribute its two breweries to the venture.

Mr Tony Portno, chairman of Bass, signed the joint venture agreement yesterday and described the investment as an "important expansion in international brewing". He saw "considerable opportunities for growth" in the Chinese beer market.

The China market, now the world's second largest behind that of the US, has been growing by more than 20 per cent a year over the past decade. China is attracting a flood of foreign investment into a fragmented industry of some 850 local and regional brewers. Consumption is 12 litres per person per year, compared with an average of 100 litres in Europe.

The UK brewer's majority stake ensures the right to appoint the general manager, and finance and technical directors. The chairman will be appointed by Ginsber.

Bass Ginsber will produce and market Tennent's Lager, one of Bass's main brands.

Financial Times, 16 May 1995

Critics of TNCs argue that the technologies they transfer are largely capital-intensive – that is, they require the use of a large amount of capital per unit of labour employed. *As a consequence, DFI creates few new jobs and prevents the use and development of more labour-intensive technologies which might be more consistent with LDC employment-creation objectives.* Whether or not TNCs can or will develop new technologies specifically suited to the economic conditions found in poorer countries remains an open question.

- **The impact of DFI on the balance of payments**

Credit items in the balance of payments (BoP) will include:

- the initial act of DFI which usually brings new capital into the host economy (although sometimes TNCs will borrow from local banks or other sources with no new capital transferred);
- exports that result from the DFI;
- a reduction in imports if the DFI is import-substituting (but see Chapter 7).

Debit items in the BoP will include:

- imports of machinery and equipment, raw materials and intermediate goods not locally available;
- payments made by the subsidiary to the parent company for technical and managerial inputs – royalties and other fees;
- the repatriation of profits made by the subsidiary back to the parent or some other part of the TNC.

Whether the net balance of payments effect of DFI is positive or negative is an empirical issue that can only be settled by looking at the data for a specific country over a given period. But this is more complicated than it seems because TNCs use *intra-corporate* or **transfer prices** on all transactions that take place within the enterprise. Such prices can differ from market prices, and TNCs will set transfer prices to meet their global corporate objectives in profit-maximization, tax-minimization, the minimization of risks, etc.

Conclusions

There always exists the potential for clashes of interest between transnational corporations and host governments. TNCs are concerned with their global objectives whereas national governments are concerned with national development objectives. It has been suggested above that conflicts might well arise with respect to technology, employment and the balance of payments.

Clearly TNCs have a broader impact on the countries they invest in. They introduce new products with their marketing and advertising techniques and create new 'lifestyles'. They may well displace traditional products and eliminate local competition, destroying old jobs as well as creating new jobs.

However, if it is the case that – as the quote from *The Economist* at the start of this chapter argues – the real power of the TNCs lies in their ownership of *knowledge*, then for the LDC the real value of direct foreign investment is the potential knowledge that it makes available to the host economy. The problem for the LDC government is to create the framework within which that knowledge is most efficiently and effectively acquired.

KEY WORDS

Intra-corporate trade	Non-equity operations
Direct foreign investment	Licensing
Parent companies	Franchising
Foreign affiliates	Internalization
Joint ventures	Neo-colonialism
Equity	Transfer prices

Reading list
Crum, R., and Davies, S., *Multinationals*, Heinemann Educational, 1991.

Essay topics
1. 'Trade, not aid'. Discuss this view on policies to promote economic development in developing economies. [20 marks]
   [University of Cambridge Local Examinations Syndicate, AS level, 1991]
2. Is a developing country more likely to have a deficit on the current account of its balance of payments than a developed country? [25 marks]
   [University of Cambridge Local Examinations Syndicate, 1991]

Chapter Ten
Aid and debt

'The goal must be to make aid a more effective weapon in the war against global poverty. This entails challenges for donors and recipients alike.' World Bank, 1990

What is foreign aid?

Foreign aid consists of transfers of real resources to LDCs on **concessional terms**. It excludes purely commercial transactions and should exclude military aid which does not have as its objective the promotion of economic development.

Aid can be given in various forms:

- as grants or loans;
- as technical assistance;
- as commodity (largely food) aid.

There may be various forms of **conditionality** attached. For example, aid may be given for a *project* (to build a road) or made available for a *programme* (to improve the transport sector).

Bilateral aid is given by the aid agency of one country (the UK Overseas Development Administration) to recipients in another.

Multilateral aid (through the EU, the World Bank or a UN agency) is usually considered superior to bilateral aid as it avoids the problems that might arise in bilateral one-to-one relationships.

Bilateral aid is normally **tied** to a particular project or programme and must be spent in the donor country. Multilateral aid may be tied to a specific project or programme but cannot require that the funds are spent in a particular country.

Aid refers only to economic assistance that qualifies as **'official development assistance'** (ODA), which is grants or loans:

- undertaken by the official sector;
- with the promotion of economic development as main objectives;
- at concessional financial terms – this involves calculation of the **grant element** of a loan (the difference between market interest rates and repayment terms and those actually charged on the loan) which must be at least 25 per cent for a loan to qualify as ODA.

Table 16 Total net resource flows to developing countries
(current US$ billion)

		1970	1975	1980	1985	1990	1991	1992	1993
I.	*Official development finance (ODF)*	8.9	18.3	34.3	44.1	70.1	69.6	70.4	68.5
	of which official development assistance (ODA)	7.9	14.9	27.3	32.9	53.1	58.3	59.5	55.2
II.	*Total export credits*	2.7	5.6	16.1	4.0	4.4	2.0	0.5	5.0
III.	*Private flows*	8.3	22.8	65.5	30.1	53.4	52.5	81.1	93.9
	(1) Direct investment (OECD)	3.7	11.4	11.2	6.5	27.2	23.4	25.1	35.0
	(2) International bank lending	3.0	8.5	49.0	15.2	15.0	11.0	31.0	9.0
	(3) Total bond lending	0.3	0.4	1.1	4.2	0.4	6.3	13.6	36.6
	(4) Other private	0.4	1.2	1.8	1.3	5.7	6.3	5.5	7.0
	(5) Grants by non-government organizations (NGOs)	0.9	1.3	2.4	2.9	5.1	5.4	5.9	6.3
	Total net resource flows I + II + III:	19.9	46.7	115.9	78.2	127.8	124.0	152.9	167.4
At 1992 prices and exchange rates:									
	Total net resource flows					146.3	140.2	131.5	152.9	170.8
	Total official development finance					82.5	76.9	73.9	70.4	69.9
	Total ODA receipts					61.5	58.4	61.9	59.5	56.3

Source: OECD Report, *Development Co-operation*, 1994

Table 16 gives details of total net resource flows to developing countries. The highlights are:

- a fall in Official Development Finance (ODF) in current prices between 1992 and 1993 (ODF includes official flows for development purposes but which have too low a grant element to qualify as aid);
- a fall in Official Development Assistance (ODA), in both current and constant prices, in part reflecting reductions in US and Japanese ODA;
- a significant fall in the share in total flows of both ODF and ODA;
- a major increase in private flows to recipient countries, especially direct foreign investment (DFI) and bond lending;
- great instability in international bank lending, with peak lending in 1980 and 1992, followed by massive reductions.

Table 17 shows changes in the composition of net resource flows. In the 1970s there was a shift towards private flows which was given added weight by the aid policies of the Reagan and Thatcher administrations. The Mexican debt crisis of 1982 and its generalization to the rest of the Third World led to a fall in private flows and an increase in

Table 17 Total net resource flows to developing countries (percentage of total)

	1970	1980	1985	1990	1993
Official development finance (ODF)	44.7	29.6	56.4	54.9	40.9
Of which: Official development assistance (ODA)	39.7	23.6	42.1	41.5	33.0
II. Total export credits	13.6	13.9	5.1	3.4	3.0
III. Private flows	41.7	56.5	38.5	41.8	56.1
Of which: International bank lending	15	42.3	19.4	21.3	5.3

the relative importance of ODF and ODA. There has been a further change between 1990 and 1993, with private flows once again accounting for more than 50 per cent of total resource flows. International bank lending, however, fluctuated between 1990 and 1993, with a peak in 1992 followed by a low in 1993.

At the end of 1994, Mexico suffered another crisis. Political instability and economic uncertainty triggered a massive outflow of capital, a fall in stock market prices and a devaluation of the peso. 1995 has witnessed attempts by the USA and the IMF to provide a financial rescue package.

Main features of the UK aid programme

Total planned ODA expenditure – comprising aid to developing countries, assistance to Eastern Europe and the former Soviet Union, and global environmental assistance – will be £2276 million in 1993–94 and £2137 million in 1995–96. Within those totals, aid for developing countries rises in 1993–94 to £1900 million, and is then frozen at that amount for 1994–95 and 1995–96.

There has been a shift from bilateral to multilateral allocations, with 23 per cent of the UK aid programme going through the EU alone in 1991.

An increasing proportion of aid is spent on *humanitarian aid*.

There have been changes in geographical allocations, with a shift to Africa. Within Asia there has been a shift away from India (still however the largest recipient) towards China and Indonesia.

Aid to developing countries now accounts for 0.31 per cent of our GNP. In the period 1979–83 the average was 0.40 per cent, and the UN 'target' is 0.70 per cent. Only four donor countries (Denmark, Norway, Sweden and the Netherlands) at present meet or exceed that target.

BRITISH AID POLICY

The major aims of UK aid are to support a number of key policy areas:

- **Economic liberalization**: to promote policy and institutional change designed to encourage the efficient operation of markets and to reform and restructure public-sector enterprises and institutions.
- **Private sector development**: provision of technical and/or financial assistance to encourage policy reform and stimulate private-sector activities.
- **Poverty reduction**: projects and programmes designed to help the poor meet their social and economic needs.
- **Human development**: to promote in-country education by improving the capacities of educational institutions and systems.
- **Women in development**: to ensure that women whose lives are affected by aid projects are properly consulted and are active participants in project implementation and that the gender aspects of development are fully integrated in the aid programme.
- **Sustainable forest management**: to promote the management of forests and trees for the sustainable supply of forest products (building materials, fuel, food, medicines, watershed protection and erosion control, timber and other products) for sale locally and internationally.

By sector, nearly 50 per cent of aid goes into *social and administrative infrastructure* (education, health, population, planning and public administration) and *economic infrastructure* (transport and communications, energy).

The aid relationship

Many economic and political issues arise in the aid relationship:

- why donors give aid;
- why poor countries accept aid;
- how aid should be given:
  - loans versus grants
  - tied versus untied aid
  - bilateral versus multilateral aid
  - project versus programme aid;
- which countries should be given aid;
- the impact of aid on the process of growth and development.

Even after 50 years' experience of aid, clear and simple answers cannot be given to these issues. Aid by itself cannot solve problems of poverty and inequality, but most people accept that aid should be made available to the poorest and most vulnerable in order to help alleviate their plight.

The debt crisis

The global debt crisis erupted in 1982 when Mexico came close to defaulting on its international obligations. In 1970, total LDC external debt had stood at $68 billion. It had risen to $635.8 billion in 1980 and in 1982 it stood at $846.6 billion. After a brief spell when it grew only slowly, growth again accelerated and the total stood at $1421 billion in 1990 and $1630 billion in 1993. The largest LDC debtors, in terms of total debt, are listed in Table 18.

However, the absolute size of a country's debt is less important than its ability to service that debt - that is, to make interest and capital repayments. With the exception of Mexico and Argentina, the largest absolute debtors do not have the highest **debt service ratios,** as shown in Table 19.

The acquisition of debt does not necessarily lead to debt problems. Borrowing increases the resources that countries have access to, and provided that those resources are used in a productive manner – that is, generate an *income* that permits the debt to be serviced – then a debt problem should not emerge. If the debt has to be repaid in a foreign currency, then clearly the resources borrowed must, directly or indirectly, generate the foreign exchange needed for repayment. In

Table 18 Top ten debtor countries in 1992

	$ million	Total debt service as % of exports of goods and services
Brazil	121.1	23.1
Mexico	113.4	44.4
Indonesia	84.4	32.1
Russian Federation	78.7	3.8
India	76.9	25.3
China	69.3	10.3
Argentina	67.6	34.4
Turkey	54.8	31.9
Poland	48.5	7.9
Republic of Korea	43.0	7.4

Source: World Bank, 1994

IS FOREIGN AID A WASTE OF MONEY?

The goal of foreign aid – at least officially – is usually to help the poor. Yet the economic logic behind this notion is surprisingly weak. Many economists argue that poor countries stay poor because they suffer from a shortage of capital. Poor people cannot save much, so poor countries cannot finance the investment that is needed for them to grow. Foreign aid is supposed to fill that gap.

This argument is dubious. First, it is unclear that developing countries really do face a capital shortage. In recent years, many of the biggest recipients of aid have enjoyed large inflows of private capital. Second, low savings rates cannot be explained by absolute poverty alone. Even the poorest countries have rich people. On average, 50 per cent of income in developing countries is held by the richest 20 per cent of the population. These rich elites could save more. Low domestic savings rates imply that they choose not to save or, more likely, choose not to save at home.

Just as economic theory cannot give a satisfactory rationale for aid, empirical evidence that it actually works is hard to find. There are examples of specific projects that have done a lot of good – an immunisation programme that cuts the rate of disease, for example. But in aggregate, economists have a tough time proving that aid has done much either to help the poor or to promote growth.

Peter Boone, an economist at the London School of Economics, has made a comprehensive study of overall aid flows to 96 countries between 1971 and 1990, and tries to test for their impact on investment and growth. The results are striking. In almost all cases aid is spent entirely on consumption. In some countries governments use aid to increase their own consumption, in others the increase occurs in private consumption; but practically nowhere is there a big increase in investment. Only in small countries where foreign aid makes up more than 15 per cent of GDP is there a significant correlation between investment and aid.

"So what?", supporters of foreign aid might ask. Higher consumption might well be a goal in itself. It might mean that the poorest were consuming more, or it could reflect higher government expenditures on education or health services. In both cases foreign aid could be making the poor better off. To test this, Mr Boone tries to measure the direct effect of foreign aid on indicators of human development.

He reckons that infant mortality is a good measure of whether conditions for the poorest are improving. If consumption goes up or health services improve, fewer babies should die. Again his results are surprising: aid flows seem to have no impact on infant mortality rates.

If foreign aid is neither promoting growth nor improving the lives of the poorest, then where is it going? Mr Boone's conclusion is that it is most probably supporting the consumption of the richest, those who least need help.

Source: *The Economist*, 10 December 1994

Table 19 Top ten debtors in 1992, on
the basis of debt service ratio

Guinea-Bissau	92.7
Algeria	71.3
Mexico	44.4
Paraguay	40.3
Uganda	40.2
Bolivia	39.0
Colombia	36.4
Burundi	35.3
Argentina	34.4
Honduras	33.7

Source: World Bank, 1994

other words, debtor countries have to run a balance-of-payments current account surplus in order to repay their debts.

Debt problems arise for a variety of reasons. Interest rates may rise and export prices fall. ODA may be reduced. Natural disasters or political instability usually lead to falls in output. Sometimes commercial banks overlend for the wrong reasons to the wrong countries/institutions/people. Governments in poor countries inadvertently or deliberately may misuse the resources that incurring debt makes available. The flight of capital from poorer to richer countries has also been a major problem in a number of countries, such as Mexico.

The debt crisis is thus a complex problem. The type of debt – private versus public, concessional versus non-concessional, short-term versus long term – varies between countries, as do the benefits that individual debtor countries have derived from the various debt alleviation schemes implemented by the international community.

Conclusions

The aid relationship is a complex one. Aid is not always given for the right reasons to the right people. It is a part of a broader political strategic picture in which the promotion of development might be secondary. It should not cause great surprise, therefore, if a clear link between aid and development cannot be demonstrated.

But this is *not* an argument against aid as such. Donors can improve the quality of the aid they give and recipients can ensure that the projects and sectors that receive aid are consistent with national development objectives. As the World Bank argues, both sides have responsibilities if aid is to become a more effective weapon in the war against poverty.

```
                         KEY WORDS

  Concessional terms        Tied aid
  Conditionality            Official development assistance
  Bilateral aid             Grant element
  Multilateral aid          Debt crisis
```

Essay topics

1. 'Nigeria's economic potential has been constrained by weak policy implementation, large fiscal deficits and a severe external debt burden' (Barclays Bank). Discuss.
   [Oxford & Cambridge Schools Examination Board 1995]
2. (a) Why is there an international debt problem in the world economy? [10 marks]
   (b) Discuss how the international banking system has sought to ease the debt problems of economies such as Mexico, Jamaica and Poland. [10 marks]
   [University of Cambridge Local Examinations Syndicate, AS level, 1995]
3. (a) Outline the main economic problems faced by poor developing countries such as those in Africa and Asia. [8 marks]
   (b) Critically assess the various ways in which the richer countries of the world can try to help the governments of the poor countries to improve the standard of living of their people. [17 marks]
   [Associated Examining Board 1994]

Data Response Question

This task is based on a question set in a specimen paper by the University of London Examinations and Assessment Council. Read the article, which is adapted from 'How to relieve Third World debt' by Michael Meacher MP, published in the *Guardian* on 28 February 1994. Then answer the questions.

Third World debt has now reached a terrifying level, in excess of a trillion pounds. Much of it is patently un-repayable, yet it is crippling economic development in countries that contain three-fifths of the world's population. The crisis is getting worse, not better: in the last two years alone these countries' debt has increased by £260 billion. It is certainly not for their lack of trying to address the issue. In 1982, the total external debt of the Third World was £550 billion. Since then, debtor countries have paid back £9,940 billion in debt service payments to creditors. Yet in 1994, they now owe £1,150 billion.

The traditional idea of the rich North supporting the poor South with regular aid flows stands on its head. Servicing debt now costs the Third World around £170 billion a year. At the same time, the world's main aid donors provide the developing countries with about £50 billion a year in aid. This reverse flow of resources now applies in the case of Britain as well. In 1990, Britain received in debt repayments £2.5 billion more than the aid it paid out. But, however perverse, doesn't this benefit Britain? But Britain may not benefit. For example, the drugs trade which so seriously threatens our culture is built on debt pressures in Latin America.

In fact the debt crisis has been brought about by factors over which developing countries have had no control: plummeting commodity prices and soaring interest rates. Of the 55 countries in sub-Saharan Africa, 48 depend on just three products – tea, cocoa and coffee – for more than half of their export earnings, yet the prices of these three commodities fell during the 1980s by more than 30 per cent. That collapse of buying power, plus very high interest rates in the 1980s, crippled them. Even so, between 1985 and 1992 Africa still repaid £55 billion in debt.

1. (a) What is meant by 'debt service payments'? [2 marks]
   (b) How may debt service payments help to explain why much Third World debt is 'patently un-repayable'? [4 marks]
2. Explain why the build-up of international debt is 'crippling economic development in countries that contain three-fifths of the world's population'. [7 marks]
3. The passage mentions one reason, related to the growth of the drugs trade, why developed countries such as Britain may also suffer indirectly from the build-up of Third World debt. Explain *one* reason why it may be in the interest of developed countries to reduce the amount of Third World debt. [5 marks]
4. Discuss appropriate policies for tackling the causes of the build-up of Third World debt. [7 marks]

Conclusion

This book has attempted to identify and discuss a relatively small number of the issues and problems currently faced by developing countries.

Economic development has been pursued by poor countries in an attempt to raise *per capita* incomes and to change the structures of production and trade largely inherited from the colonial period.

Some countries have succeeded in this task and valuable insights can be drawn from their experiences. Other countries have been less successful, and massive problems remain with regard to poverty, inequality, unemployment and, increasingly, environmental degradation. There is no single model of development, however, and country-specific strategies and policies cannot be simplistically transferred to other countries with different histories, structures, institutions and cultures.

One of the main arguments presented in the book is that industrialization is a necessary, but not sufficient, condition, for high and sustained rates of growth of *per capita* income and structural transformation. The modernization of the agricultural sector is of strategic importance in this respect.

The emergence of the NICs presents an example of successful industrialization. There are conflicting explanations as to why some East and South East Asian economies have been so successful, with debate focusing on the balance between the market on the one hand and state intervention on the other. The extent to which developing countries can emulate the success of the NICs remains an open question.

The majority of social scientists who study the development of poor countries accept that it is a complex, multidimensional process. Historical, institutional, social and political factors all need to be taken into account in order that we are able to reach a better understanding of the processes of growth and development.

Terminology is thus important because it colours the way that we consider problems of global poverty and inequality and formulate policies for their alleviation.

Suggested reading

- Annual reports

The World Bank publishes both an *Annual Report* (free) and the annual *World Development Report*, published by Oxford University

Press for the World Bank. It has been published annually since 1978 and each year now has a theme (Poverty, Environment, Employment, etc.). The United Nations' Conference on Trade and Development (UNCTAD) publishes an annual *Trade and Development Report* and *The Least Developed Countries Report* (both free). *Finance and Development* is the quarterly publication of the IMF and the World Bank (free). The European Union (EU) publishes *The Courier* (free), containing a wealth of material on the ACP (African, Pacific and Caribbean) countries. The United Nations' Development Programme (UNDP) publishes an annual *Human Development Report* (Oxford University Press for the United Nations).

- Aid statistics

Aid statistics are to be found in the OECD's annual *Development Co-operation Report* (OECD, Paris, free).

- Other publications

Oxfam has published *The Oxfam Poverty Report* (1995), which is a good indication of the non-governmental organization (NGO) view of development. The Overseas Development Institute (ODI) in London publishes a series of invaluable *Briefing Papers*. *The Economist* and *The Financial Times* publish many articles dealing with Third World issues, especially on commodities, international business and finance.

Index